A Conservation Bibliography

for

Librarians, Archivists, and Administrators

by

Carolyn Clark Morrow

and

Steven B. Schoenly

The Whitston Publishing Company
Troy, New York
1979

PREFACE

The field of conservation of library and archival materials has been hampered from the beginning by the seemingly insurmountable prospect of millions of simultaneously deteriorating documents; a dearth of programs for treatment; lack of specialized personnel and training facilities; and the inability of technology to provide all the answers and the means for inexpensive, mass treatment.

To add to this confusion, the literature of book and document conservation is diverse, drawing from the allied fields of librarianship, archives and manuscripts, management, commercial bookbinding, fine binding, museology, art restoration, chemistry, micrographics, publishing, photography, architecture, systems engineering, psychology, and even law enforcement. This bibliography is an attempt to draw together this diverse information for the use of those studying conservation, or in a position to affect conservation policy in an institution or repository. Part I is a classified, annotated bibliography of selected resources from the literature of conservation arranged in reverse chronological order within each section. The citations were selected for Part I on the basis of their applicability to the major themes/problems in the field. Since library and archives conservation is a relatively new field, more has been written—and more importantly, more is known—about some topics than others. However, an attempt was made to cover, as well as possible within the existing literature, each important topic. Part II is a comprehensive bibliography of the literature since 1966. Citations are listed in alphabetical order and entries included in Part I are repeated in Part II. The subject index to Part II covers topics more specific than those in Part I and includes see references.

The bibliography cites literature which has appeared since 1966 because that was the year of the flood in Florence, Italy, when conservators from all over the world participated in salvage and restoration efforts, attesting to an international commitment to the preservation of cultural property. Techniques developed as a result of the flood (because of its mammoth proportions and the need for immediate action) have had a great impact on those methods and attitudes which are developing to meet the present and future problems of deteriorating paper collections.

Carolyn Clark Morrow
Southern Illinois University
at Carbondale

Steven Schoenly
The University of Mississippi

A Conservation Bibliography

TABLE OF CONTENTS

Part I

A

Conservation Administration

A 1   The Organization of Conservation Functions

A 1.1   Darling, Pamela W. "Books in peril; a local preservation program: where to start." *Library Journal*   101 (November 15, 1976): 2343-47. illus.

> Plea for initiation of conservation programs in libraries. Includes components of a broad preservation program, strategy for evaluating preservation needs and establishing priorities, and implementation.

A 1.2   Shelley, Karen Lee. "The future of conservation in research libraries." *Journal of Academic Librarianship* 1, 6 (January 1976): 15-18.

> Justification for the position of conservation librarian in research libraries and development of a conservation program. Administrative structure for the conservation function.

A 1.3   Walker, Gay. "Preservation efforts in larger U.S. academic libraries." *College and Research Libraries* 36 (January 1975): 39-44.

> Results of a survey of preservation activities in large U. S. academic libraries. Recommendations for establishing a preservation unit.

A 1.4   Baker, John P. "Restoration of library materials: some administrative considerations." *Library Scene* 3, 4 (December 1974): 4-6.

> Defines the problem of deteriorating library collections, describes the conservation division of the New York Public Library, and identifies principles basic in managing a restoration program.

A 1.5   Rogers, Rutherford D. and David C. Weber. "Binding and preservation." In *University Library Administration* (New York: Wilson, 1971), pp. 184-92.

Notes the function of binding and preservation in a research library, mentions policies, choice of binderies, budgeting, staff. Briefly describes a comprehensive preservation program and its inclusion in an administrative organization. Significant for the fact that the concept is included in a standard text on library administration. Though its description does not fit what actually occurs, the basic principles are expounded.

A 1.6   Smith, Richard D. "Guidelines for preservation." *Special Libraries* 59, 5 (May-June 1968): 346-52.

Recommends a written policy which meets objectives of each library and falls within its financial and staff resources. Best for its basic discussion of the causes of paper deterioration.

A 1.7   Poole, Frazer G. "The research library and book conservation." *Bollettino dell'Istituto di Patologia del Libro* 29 (January-December 1970): 99-122.

Sketches the historical background of the problem of deteriorating book paper. Describes the Library of Congress preservation program, including its organization, functions, budgeting, and personnel.

A 1.8   Williams, Gordon R. "The preservation of deteriorating books. (1) Examination of the problem. (2) Recommendations for a solution." *Library Journal* 91 (January 1, 1966): 51-56; 91 (January 15, 1966): 189-94.

Defines the scope of the preservation problem, and indicates that the solution is a federally supported central agency to assure the physical preservation of at least one example of every deteriorating record.

A 1.9   Barr, Pelham. "Book Conservation and university library administration." *College and Research Libraries* 7 (July 1946): 214-19.

Landmark argument for a comprehensive conservation program. Suggests that the "polite neglect" of book conservation has been an error on the part of university librarians. Principles outlined are relevant today.

A 2 *Conservation Policy*

A 2.1   International Association of Music Libraries. Research Libraries Commission. *Conservation in Music Libraries.* London: International Association of Music Libraries, 1977. 20 pp., bibliog.

Conservation policy statement specifically designed for use in music libraries. Discusses problems, principles of treatment, and techniques and remedies. Brief mention of long term considerations.

A 2.2   Belanger, Terry. "The price of preservation." *Times Literary Supplement*, no. 3947 (November 18, 1977): 1358-59.

Typifies the acquisition philosophy of north American college and university libraries as "more is better" and accuses them of not being willing or able to preserve what they so enthusiastically and indiscriminately collected in the easy-money '70s.

A 2.3   University of Wisconsin-Madison Library System. Preservation of Library Materials Committee. *Statement on the Conservation of Library Materials.* Madison: University of Wisconsin-Madison Library System, 1976. 14 pp., bibliog.

Library committee statement on components of a preservation program. One of the few existing statements. Very general and unfortunately theoretical. More plea than policy.

A 2.4   Brock, Jo Ann. *A Program for the Preservation of Library Materials in the General Library.* Berkeley: University of California Library, 1975. 45 pp.

Defines broad problems of book conservation, summarizes results of current research, outlines organizational pattern of existing conservation departments as a basis for assigning priorities and requesting funding. Attempts a cost estimate.

A 2.5   Henderson, James W. *Memorandum on Conservation of the Collections.* New York: The New York Public Library, 1970. 28 pp.

> First comprehensive, systematically organized statement on library conservation. Includes specific recommendations for a conservation program at NYPL. Appendices list conservation programs in priority order.

A 3 Professionalization, Education, and Training

A 3.1   American Library Association. Resources and Technical Services Division. Committee on Preservation of Library Materials. *Preservation Training and Information.* Chicago: American Library Association, 1977. 2 pp.

Result of questionnaires sent to accredited library schools, paper/book workshops, and related organizations. Lists academic courses, available course outlines and information, and related educational possibilities. Updated annually.

A 3.2   Banks, Paul N. *Professional Training in Library and Archives Conservation.* Chicago: The Newberry Library, 1975. 4 pp.

Advice to people attempting to enter the field of book conservation. Briefly defines the field, related fields, types of personnel involved in conservation, and steps to be taken by a prospective conservator.

A 3.3   Morrison, Robert C. "Experience in restoration; a workshop-seminar conducted by the New England Document Conservation Center." *Library Scene* 5 (June 1976): 30-31.

Description of conference sponsored by the Library Binding Institute and conducted by the New England Document Conservation Center. Topics covered included nature of library materials, causes of deterioration, techniques of conservation, and disaster planning. Description of "hands-on" workshop for participants with "only a little knowledge of the concepts and eager to learn all they could about this newly emerging field."

A 3.4   Banks, Paul N. "The librarian as conservator." *Library Quarterly* 40, 1 (January 1970): 192-98.

Defines book conservation; lists qualifications of a book conservator relating them to those of a scientist, craftsman, administrator, and book collector; compares book conservation with art conservation; mentions the role of conservator in the library and the education of conservators.

A 3.5   Henderson, James W. and Robert G. Krupp. "The Librarian as conservator." *Library Quarterly* 40, 1 (January 1970): 176-91.

Considers the role of librarians as administrators of library conservation. Historical and technical background of conservation. Organization and management of a conservation program.

A 3.6   Banks, Paul N. "The scientist, the scholar and the book conservator: some thoughts on book conservation as a profession." *Atti Della XLIX Riunione della S.I.P.S.*, Siena, 23-27   Settembre, 1967 (September 1967): 1213-19.

A 4   Cooperation

A 4.1   Brahm, Walter. "A regional approach to conservation: the New England Document Conservation Center." *American Archivist* 40 (October 1977): 421-27.

> Describes steps which lead to the establishment of the New England Document Conservation Center by the New England Library Board, development of a preliminary budget for start-up equipment and staff, fund-raising, staffing, types of service, and growth and accomplishments. Endorsement of the regional concept in conservation services.

A 4.2   Library of Congress. "Report on a planning conference for a national preservation program, Washington, D. C., December 16-17, 1976." *Library of Congress Information Bulletin* 36 (February 18, 1977): 129-31.

> Discusses major conference themes—costs, personnel, and training and outlines the overwhelming size of the preservation problem. Names participants in the conference and their paper topics. *Proceedings* of the Conference will be distributed to conferencees and subsequently published.

A 4.3   Darling, Pamela W. "Preservation: a national plan at last?" *Library Journal* 102 (February 15, 1977): 447-49.

> Report on the two-day National Preservation Program Planning Conference. Outlines the purpose of the conference, participants, and their speeches. Description of sessions and main topics covered, including the elements of a national program and the role of scientific research for preservation.

A 4.4   Banks, Paul N. "Books in peril; cooperative approaches to conservation." *Library Journal* 101 (November 15, 1976): 2348-51.

> Discusses the qualitative, quantitative, and economic dimensions of the conservation problem as a context for recommending

cooperation in the areas of personnel, reproduction of materials, treatment, and facilities. Notes possible organizational structures.

A 4.5	National Conservation Advisory Council. *Conservation of Cultural Property in the United States.* Washington, D. C.: NCAC, 1976. 42 pp.

Summary of national needs in conservation, including training personnel, educating users of services, increasing facilities, encouraging research, and developing standards. Also includes recommendations for national conservation planning, definitions of terms used in the report, objectives, and list of members of NCAC. Intended to bring together needs in the conservation of cultural property in museums, libraries, and historical buildings. See also *Report of the Study Committee on Libraries and Archives,* 1978.

A 4.6	National Conservation Advisory Council. *Report from the Regional Centers Study Committee to the National Conservation Advisory Council.* Washington, D. C.: NCAC, 1976. 25 pp.

Although addressed to art museums and historical agencies, relevant for description of characteristics of regional facilities, including advantages, guidelines, locations, and costs.

A 4.7	Wieder, Joachim. "The restoration and conservation of library and archive materials as an international task." *IFLA Journal* 1, 1 (February 1975): 21-29.

Historical review of international cooperative conservation. Discusses requirements for future international cooperation in coordinating activities, preventing duplication of effort, exchanging information, and developing standards. Outlines training programs and models for regional and interstate cooperation.

A 4.8	Buck, Richard D. "On conservation; what is a regional conservation center and why?" *Museum News* 52, 8 (May 1974): 10.

Briefly defines the concept of a regional conservation center.

A 4.9   Haas, Warren J. *Preparation of Detailed Specifications for a National System for the Preservation of Library Materials.* Washington, D.C.: Association of Research Libraries, 1972. Reprinted in *Information—Part 2: Reports, Bibliographies* 2, 1-2 (1973): 17-37.

Identifies specific steps to be taken by organizations and libraries to resolve the problem of deteriorating library collections. Includes causes of paper deterioration and remedial techniques, methods of text preservation, and approaches to collective action in areas of standards, identification and recording of preservation copies, and priorities.

A 4.10   Nordstrand, Ove K. "The conference on the international cooperation for the preservation of the book, Florence, 12-14 March 1970." *Restaurator* 1, 3 (1970): 214-20.

Summaries of papers given at the conference, including discussion of an international center for preservation, research, training, cooperation during the restoration at BNCP. Description of mass preservation system based on assembly line concept. Historical development of library conservation in the U.S. Focuses on the organizational and administrative aspects of book preservation.

A 5 Programs and Facilities

A 5.1 New York Public Library. *Report 1976/77.* New York: New York Public Library, 1977. illus.

> A remarkable statement expressing the immediacy of the conservation problem in the form of an annual report. For special emphasis printed on ordinary newsprint. Describes bibliocide in the Library.

A 5.2 Ogden, Sherelyn J. B. "Conservation of library materials at The Newberry Library." *Guild of Bookworkers Journal* 14, 1 (1975): 11-14. illus.

> Background of the development of Newberry's conservation program. Describes present organization, personnel, projects, and mentions types of treatments performed. Low-key presentation of what is without question a pace-setting program in the field of library conservation.

A 5.3 "Preservation research program of the Library of Congress." *Library of Congress Information Bulletin* 31, 37 (September 15, 1972): A165-68. illus.

> Describes reorganization of the LC preservation program to provide a research laboratory. Lists research projects underway, including neutralization and buffering of paper, mass deacidification, strengthening of paper, treatment of flood damaged materials, adhesive stains, storage containers for microfilm, substitutes for lamination, atmospheric conditions leading to deterioration of paper, and procedures for screening recommendations for research.

A 5.4 Rozkova, Galina S. "Hygiene and restoration of book stock at libraries; some points of interest regarding the work of the Lenin State Library of the USSR." *Restaurator* 1, 3 (1970): 191-97.

> Description of work since 1944 in the Lenin State Library's Department of Book Hygiene and Restoration, including

research; principle tasks of preservation of the book stock; methodological assistance to other libraries and public institutions; and the structure, functions, and activities of the department.

A 5.5   Shaffer, Norman J. "Library of Congress pilot preservation project." *College and Research Libraries* 30 (January 1969): 5-11.

Discusses the background, operation, and findings of the LC pilot preservation project. Outlines the feasibility of locating and listing the best copies of deteriorating titles. Includes forms used for a "book condition report," estimates of time and costs of locating titles, and implications of the project for a national preservation collection.

Part I

B

Environmental Protection

B 1 *Environmental Hazards*

B 1.1 Watson, A. J. "Manufacturing and environmental factors affecting the permanence of paper." *Archives and Manuscripts* 6, 7 (August 1976): 285-91.

Description of paper-making processes and components in relation to permanent/durable paper, environmental factors, and artificial aging.

B 1.2 Wessel, Carl J. "Environmental factors affecting the permanence of library materials." *Library Quarterly* 40, 1 (January 1970): 39-84.

Focuses on the conditions present in American urban research libraries. Suggestions for environmental controls. Includes tables.

B 1.3 Smith, Richard D. "Paper impermanence as a consequence of pH and storage conditions." *Library Quarterly* 39, 2 (April 1969): 153-95.

Outlines historical (nineteenth and twentieth century) background of paper impermanence. Discusses action of air pollution, temperature, and inferior storage conditions. Includes pH table.

B 1.4 Stolow, Nathan. "The action of environment on museum objects. Part I: humidity, temperature, atmospheric pollution." *Curator* 9, 3 (September 1966): 175-85. diagrams.

Discussion of the damaging factors and how to measure, record, regulate, and compensate for them. Relationship between temperature, moisture, and relative humidity. Outlines the dangers to humidity-sensitive materials, the action of pollution and its relation to relative humidity and temperature. Includes definition of microclimatology.

B 1.5   Stolow, Nathan. "The action of environment on museum objects. Part II: light." *Curator* 9, 4 (December 1966): 298-306. diagrams.

Reviews the major issues in deterioration from photochemical activity. Notes the susceptability of exhibits. Describes systems of illumination satisfying both display and preservation requirements. Summarizes and reviews the theory and terminology of light, factors in deterioration, control of lighting, importance of taking light measurements, aesthetic problems.

B 2.1   National Conservation Advisory Council. *Statement on the Control of Environmental Conditions for Preservation of Cultural Property in Situations of Energy Shortage.* Washington, D. C.: NCAC, 1977. 2 pp. Also published in *Special Libraries* 68, 11 (November 1977): 419-20, and in *Society of American Archivists Newsletter*, September 1977, pp. 12-13.

Statement asserting the importance of repository control over internal climatic conditions. Guidelines for emergency measures in energy shortage situations.

B 2.2   Public Archives of Canada. *A Guide to the Preservation of Archival Materials.* Quebec: Minister of Supplies and Services, 1977. 16 pp.

Humorous photographs illustrating the most obvious causes of damage to archival materials by patron and staff mishandling. Intended for distribution in the reading room.

B 2.3   Torrance, J. S.   "A justification of air-conditioning in libraries." *Journal of Librarianship* 7, 3 (July 1975): 199-206.

Argues in favor of air-conditioning over mechanical ventilation in the context of recognized need for energy conservation. Discusses building design and planning, including ceiling height, lighting levels, ventilation systems. Advocates separate book and patron areas.

B 2.4   Library of Congress. *Environmental Protection of Books and Related Materials.* Washington, D. C.: Library of Congress, 1975. (Preservation Leaflet Series, No. 2) 4 pp.

Overview of the major problems in environmental protection. Includes recommended references and sources of supplies.

B 2.5   Banks, Paul N. "Environmental standards for storage of books and manuscripts." *Library Journal* 99 (February 1, 1974): 339-43.

Summary of factors in building planning that can influence the preservation and deterioration of library materials. Specific recommendations for levels of temperature, humidity, air impurities, lighting. Outlines requirements for exhibitions, shelving and transportation, storage of microfilm, disaster control, and monitoring systems.

B 2.6   Tombor, Tibor. "Edificio e preservazione; considerazioni sulla consezione dell'edificio di una biblioteca di conservazione" ("Building and preservation; considerations in building a library to insure book preservation"). *Bollettino dell'Istituto di Patologia del Libro* 30 (January-June 1971): 101-112.

Factors to consider in the design of a building to promote preservation.

B 2.7   Metcalf, Keyes D. "The design of book stacks and the preservation of books." *Restaurator* 1, 2 (1969): 115-25.

Historical background of library stacks design, including ventilation and temperature as a result of book stack design, air filtering, air conditioning, fire risks, sprinkling systems, prevention of fire and water damage, and causes of paper deterioration.

B 2.8   Feller, Robert L. "Control of deteriorating effects of light on museum objects: heating effects of illumination by incandescent lamps." *Museum News* 46, 9 (May 1968): 39-47.

Reviews experimental studies of the heating effects of museum lighting and cites principles in the control of the deteriorating effects of light. Technical graphs and tables.

B 2.8   Cameron, Duncan. "Environmental control: a theoretical solution." *Museum News* 46, 9 (May 1968): 17-21.

Outlines a philosophy of environmental control. Lists environ-

mental factors which must be taken into consideration in the
planning of an art museum. Discusses planning of the storage
area and the relationships of other environments to storage,
including features and requirements of such storage spaces.

B 2.10   Nelson, Elmer R. "Do we understand museum air conditioning?" *Curator* 11 (1968): 127-36.

Discusses variables in air conditioning systems for museums,
including object humidity, temperature and humidity, air
pollution, and system capacities. Advocates early involvement
in design and planning of buildings and systems.

B 2.11   Kurth, William H. and Ray W. Grim. *Moving a Library.*
New York: Scarecrow Press, 1966.   220 pp.,   illus.,
plans.

Administrative and physical aspects of moving library materials.
Chronology of operation and master plan for moving.

B 3.1   Cornell University Libraries. *CUL Emergency Manual.* Ithaca, New York: Cornell University Libraries, 1977.

Specific guidelines and procedures to deal with emergency conditions.

B 3.2   Cunha, George M. "An evaluation of recent developments for the mass drying of books." In John C. Williams, ed., *Preservation of Paper and Textiles of Historical and Artistic Value* (Washington, D. C.: American Chemical Society, 1977). (Advances in Chemistry Series, no. 164)

Discusses hypothetical costs of rehabilitation by presently available methods; briefly describes current applications, including air drying, vacuum drying, freeze drying, microwave drying, dielectric energy drying, and solvent extraction of water. Evaluates applications.

B 3.3   General Services Administration.   Accident and Fire Protection Division. Advisory Committee on the Protection of Archives and Records Centers. *Protecting Federal Records Centers From Fire.* Washington, D. C.: Government Printing Office, 1977. bibliog., illus., appendices.

Technical report of the 1973 St. Louis Records Center fire. Recommendations for limiting fire damage.

B 3.4   Meneray, Wilbur E. *Tulane University Disaster Plan.* New Orleans: Research and Publications Committee of the Library Department, 1977. 7 pp.

Policy for dealing with disasters. Describes specific dangers and priority of salvage procedures. Appendix gives sources of supplies and costs.

B 3.5   Morris, John. *Managing the Library Fire Risk.* Berkeley: University of California Office of Insurance and Risk Management, 1975. 101 pp., photos, bibliog.

> Historical and current treatment of fire risk in libraries with emphasis on automatic systems for detention and extinguishment. Includes discussion of sprinkler systems, water damage, salvage and restoration, Halon 1301 (applications for rare books and special collections), and disaster prepardedness.

B 3.6   Waters, Peter. *Procedures for Salvage of Water-Damaged Library Materials.* Washington, D. C.: Library of Congress, 1975. (Library of Congress Publications on Conservation of Library Materials) 30 pp.

> Policy and procedures designed to save a maximum amount of material with a minimum amount of restoration and replacement. Includes assessment of damage and salvage planning, effect of water on books and unbound materials, stabilization techniques, restoration techniques, and evaluation of losses. Appendices give sources, supplies, and equipment.

B 3.7   Stender, Walter W. and Evans Walker. "The National Personnel Records Center fire: a study in Disaster." *American Archivist* 37 (October 1974): 521-49. illus.

> Description of the fire, damage, salvage and reclamation efforts, and long-term effects.

B 3.8   Sellers, David Y. and Richard Strassberg. "Anatomy of a library emergency: how the Cornell University Libraries dealt with flood damages and developed plans to handle future emergencies." *Library Journal* 98 (October 1, 1973): 2824-27. illus.

> Discusses a single type of emergency-flooding, and details the successes and failures of one large library.

B 3.9   Waters, Peter.   "Book restoration after the Florence floods." *Penrose Annual* 62 (1969): 83-93. illus.

Describes the damage done by the Florence flood, and the measures taken to restore the damaged works.

B 3.10   Tribolet, Harold W.   "Restoration in Florence." *Manuscripts* 20, 4 (Fall 1968): 20-36.

Account of the author's two visits to Florence. First to help with the initial rescue and restoration efforts and then to evaluate the progress of the restoration work and make recommendations to improve the techniques in use.

B 3.11   Hamlin, Arthur T.   "Library crisis in Italy." *Library Journal* 92 (July 1967): 2516-22. illus.

Places the blame partly on the pre-flood situation. Discusses the implications of inaction and inept action by the Italian government and long-standing disregard of the needs of the nation's libraries. Outlines pre-flood situation, the scope of the disaster salvage operation, recovery efforts since the flood, and the future of the Biblioteca Nazionale Centrale.

B 4 Mutilation and Vandalism

B 4.1   Walch, Timothy. *Archives and Manuscripts: Security.* Chicago: Society of American Archivists, 1977. 30 pp. (Basic Manual Series)

Emphasis on security/theft but several sections are pertinent to conservation including, identification of high risk items, security against fire and flood, and archival security and the law. Appendix 2, a Model Law Relating to Library Theft (based on shoplifting statutes), has implications for a law dealing with mutilation and vandalism.

B 4.2   Kesler, Elizabeth Gates. "A Campaign against mutilation." *Journal of Academic Librarianship* 3, 1 (March 1977): 29-30.

Describes a campaign consisting of exhibits, buttons, articles, letters. Gives a faculty senate resolution and evaluates the effectiveness of the campaign.

B 4.3   Culp, R. W. "Thefts, mutilations, and library exhibits." *Special Libraries* 67, 11 (December 1976): 582-84. illus.

Discusses library mutilation and theft, ethical and economic aspects of the problem, comments on philosophical approaches to deterrents and penalties, recommends "sensitizing" the patrons to the problems through the use of exhibits. Describes exhibits which stress relevance and humor.

B 4.4   Souter, G. H. "Delinquent readers: a study of the problem in university libraries." *Journal of Academic Librarianship* 8, 2 (April 1976): 96-110.

Attempts quantification of the problems of overborrowing, retaining after recall, stealing, and mutilation. Lists types of delinquency, factors that encourage reader delinquency, and characteristics of delinquent readers.

B 4.5   Richmond, Michael L.   "Attitudes of law librarians to theft and mutilation control methods." *Law Library Journal* 68, 1 (February 1975): 60-70.

Presents results of a survey on library theft, mutilation, controls, and law librarians' attitudes toward strategies. Discusses economic and legal aspects of surveillance systems.

B 4.6   Murfin, Marjorie E. and Clyde Hendrick.   "Ripoffs tell their story: interviews with mutilators in a university library." *Journal of Academic Librarianship* 1, 2 (May 1975): 8-12.

Reports of three interviews with students who have mutilated periodicals. Reveals attitudes, motivations, frustrations, methods, temptation periods, misconceptions concerning cost of replacement, use of study carrels and penknives, and sacredness of books as opposed to journals. Maintains that a marked change in attitudes occurs when students are told the facts of time and cost of replacement.

B 4.7   Hendrick, Clyde and Marjorie E. Murfin.   "Project library ripoff: a study of periodical mutilation in a university library." *College and Research Libraries* 35 (November 1974): 402-11.

Results of a questionnaire to assess students' knowledge and attitudes about periodical mutilation. Statistics reveal few differences between mutilators and non-mutilators. Suggestions for preventative measures include publicity campaigns and specific penalty warning signs.

B 4.8   Martin, Ron G.   "Microforms and periodical mutilation." *Microform Review* 2 (January 1973): 6-8.

Presents statistics from the author's 1972 study of 92 libraries' experiences with mutilation of periodicals and use of microforms as a solution for replacement.

B 4.9   Feret, Barbara L.   "Back to student rip-offs: a point of sale." *Wilson Library Bulletin* 47 (September 1972): 46-47.

Describes educational program to help students realize the effect of mutilation and theft of library materials.

B 4.10   Lightfoot, Robert M., Jr. "Project mutilation: an attempt at a solution to a growing problem." *Illinois Libraries* 52 (November 1970): 946-49.

> Campaign to locate instances of mutilated journal articles. Cooperation with area libraries for obtaining photocopy replacements. (Photocopy replacements not tipped in but kept at desk.)

B 4.11   Hoppe, Ronald A. and Edward C. Simmel. "Book tearing and the bystander in the university library." *College and Research Libraries* 30 (May 1969): 247-51.

> Study tabulated student reactions to a mutilation occurring right next to them as an indication of how seriously students regard the crime of mutilation. Suggests little or no group peer pressure as a deterrent to mutilation.

B 5 Exhibition

B 5.1   British Standards Institution. *Recommendations for the Storage and Exhibition of Archival Documents.* London: British Standards Institution, 1977. 11 pp.

Specific and detailed standards.

B 5.2   Stolow, Nathan. "Conservation policy and the exhibition of museum collections." *Journal of the American Institute for Conservation* 16, 2 (February 1977): 12-20.

Describes conservation problems associated with the exhibition and transportation of museum collections, including problems with buildings, their environment, and condition report standards. Recommends a position of Exhibition Conservator.

B 5.3   Weiss, Susan E. "Proper exhibition lighting: protecting collections from damage." *Technology and Conservation* 1 (Spring 1977): 20-25. illus.

Describes the effect of light on exhibit objects, methods for measuring light energy, the principle of reciprocity in photodegradation, material prone to light damage, and techniques for protecting exhibits.

B 5.4   Oddy, W. A. "An unsuspected danger in display." *Museums Journal* 73, 1 (June 1973): 27-28. illus.

Discusses damage to objects placed on exhibit which can be caused by materials used in construction of exhibition cases. Advocates sample testing to avoid unexpected deterioration.

B 5.5   Werner, Anthony E. "Conservation and display: environmental control." *Museums Journal* 72, 2 (September 1972): 58-60.

Discusses air pollution and other avoidable dangers to displayed items.

B 5.6   Padfield, Tim. "The control of relative humidity and air pollution in show-cases and picture frames." *Studies in Conservation* 11 (1966): 8-30.

Discusses the use of humidity-sensitive materials to stabilize relative humidity in exhibit environments. Mentions atmospheric moisture, effect of RH changes on museum objects, air flow and air leakage, effect of temperature on RH, and methods of maintaining a constant RH.

Part I

C

Information Preservation

C 1 Storage and Handling of Film

C 1.1   McDermott, Jack C. "Unique applications: critical material storage facilities." *Journal of Micrographics* 11, 3 (January-February 1978): 165-68. illus.

Emphasizes the importance of proper storage facilities for paper documents, microfilm, and computer tapes. Discusses design considerations in new buildings, security and fire protection, furniture, and environmental controls.

C 1.2   Darling, Pamela W. "Microforms in libraries: preservation and storage." *Microform Review* 5, 2 (April 1976): 93-100.

Discusses the preservation of information in microform and preservation of microforms themselves.

C 1.3   Haverling, S. "Technical aspects of the preservation of archival (security) microfilm." *UNESCO Bulletin for Libraries* 29 (March-April 1975): 68-74.

Results of an analysis by the Swedish Committee for Conservation of Source Material of the problems of preserving archival microfilm as a basis for a transition from original documents to copies on microfilm. Includes a technical description of the investigation and recommendations for preservation.

C 1.4   Library of Congress. Photoduplication Service. "Permanence of library microforms; who is responsible? Recommendations for storage of permanent record microfilm." *Microform Review* 3, 4 (October 1974): 248.

Formal statement (with reference to ANSI Standard PH5.4-1970) by the LC Photoduplication Service concerning the proper temperature and humidity ranges for storage of microfilm.

C 1.5   National Archives and Records Service. "Care of microfilm and microfilm readers." *American Archivist* 37
(April 1974): 314-15.

> Quotation from NARS General Information Leaflet, no. 24
> specifying maintenance procedures for readers which will
> promote microfilm life. Includes brief discussion of test proce-
> dures and advisable environmental conditions for readers and
> microfilm.

C 1.6   Eastman Kodak Company. *Storage and Preservation of
Microfilms.* Rochester, New York: Eastman Kodak
Company, 1972. (Kodak publication D-31.) 12 pp.,
bibliog.

> Discusses types of film, storage hazards and protection, proces-
> sing for permanence, handling, filing, and inspection. Table in
> summary form of requirements for storage and preservation of
> microfilm.

C 2 Standards, Specifications, and Processing

C 2.1   Avedon, Don M. "Microfilm generation and polarity terminology." *Special Libraries* 68 (April 1977): 141-44.

> Terminology of producing and using duplicate and master microforms. Describes a system for identifying generation and polarity. Discusses four duplicating films. Glossary of terms.

C 2.2   National Micrographics Association. *Basic U.S. Micro-graphic Standards and Specifications.* Silver Spring, Maryland: National Micrographics Association, 1976. 454 pp. illus.

> A collection of U.S. Military and Federal micrographic standards and specifications. Includes detailed requirements for film characteristics, formats, reduction ratios, density, duplication, inspection, packing and shipping, and equipment. Cites pertinent ANSI Standards and handbooks.

C 2.3   D'Alleyrand, Marc R. "Microfilming continuous tone materials." *American Archivist* 39 (October 1976): 515-19. illus.

> Techniques for microfilming documents when different shades or colors of text or background exist on the same page.

C 2.4   National Archives and Records Service. Office of Records Management. *Microfilming Records.* Washington, D. C.: The Office, 1974. 168 pp., illus.

> Discusses microfilm technology, systems, and applications, including procedures for the implementation and operation of a microfilming program. Photographs of and specifications concerning microfilm cameras, readers, and printers. Briefly outlines storage and preservation guidelines.

C 2.5   Veaner, Allen B. "Microreproduction and micropublication technical standards: what they mean to you, the user." *Microform Review* 3, 2 (April 1974): 80-84. Revision of article with similar title which appeared in *Choice* 5 (September 1968): 7.

> Discusses in layman's terms the ANSI standards which are relevant to the use of microforms in libraries, including film stock, processing chemicals, filming standards, and tests for sharpness and legibility.

C 2.6   Avedon, Don M. *NMA Standard Glossary of Micrographics.* Silver Spring, Maryland: National Micrographics Association, 1973. 71 pp.

> Standard terminology for micrographic technology, equipment, and processes. Terms that are trademarks are identified by the symbol.

C 2.7   Library of Congress. Photoduplication Service. *Specifications for the Microfilming of Books and Pamphlets in the Library of Congress.* Washington, D. C.: Library of Congress, 1973. 16 pp., glossary

> Recommended procedures for filming of monographs and pamphlets including preparation, technical considerations, filming, processing, inspection, types of copies, and storage.

C 2.8   Library of Congress. Photoduplication Service. *Specifications for the Microfilming of Newspapers in the Library of Congress.* Washington, D. C.: Library of Congress, 1972. 17 pp., glossary

> Covers preparation of newspapers for filming, filming procedures, processing, inspection, and storage.

C 2.9   Avedon, Don M. "Microfilm permanence and archival quality: standards." *Special Libraries* 63, 12 (December 1972): 586-88. Reprinted from *Journal of Micrographics* 6, 2 (November-December 1972).

> Discusses the standards for microfilm permanence and archival quality and storage conditions.

C 3 Programs and Policies

C 3.1   Hawken, William R. "Making big ones out of little ones: current trends in micrographics." *Library Journal* 102 (October 15, 1977): 2127-31.

> Discusses advantages and disadvantages of microforms as methods of storing, preserving, and disseminating information. Mentions use and functions of microforms, aspects of reader dissatisfaction, and inadequacies of reader/printers.

C 3.2   Napier, Paul A. "Developments in copying, micrographies, and graphic communications, 1976." *Library Resources and Technical Services* 21, 3 (Summer 1977): 187-215. bibliog.

> Surveys the events and literature concerning the fields named in the title for 1976.

C 3.3   Diaz, Albert J., ed. *Microforms in Libraries: A Reader.* Weston, Conn.: Microform Review, Inc., 1975.

> Numerous articles, many of them reprinted from other sources, concerning the history of micropublishing, user reactions to microforms, hardware, storage, cataloguing, standards and specifications. Includes bibliographies.

C 3.4   LaHood, Charles G., Jr. and Robert C. Sullivan. *Reprographic Services in Libraries: Organization and Administration.* Chicago: American Library Association, 1975. (Library Technology Program Publication No. 19) 74 pp.

> Administrator's guide to reprographic services in libraries including a brief account of historical development, suggestions for types of services, equipment and staff needs, and guidelines for bibliographical and technical considerations. Checklist of kinds of policies and factors to consider in establishing policies.

C 3.5   Diaz, Albert J. "Microform information sources: publications and hardware." *Microform Review* 4, 4 (October 1975): 250-61. bibliog.

> Article adapted from *Microforms in Libraries: A Reader.* Lists and discusses sources of information concerning the availability of micropublications and microform hardware for libraries.

C 3.6   American Library Association. Resources and Technical Services Division. Resources Section. Reprinting Committee. "Policy on lending to reprint and microform publishers." *Library Resources and Technical Services* 19, 2 (Spring 1975): 178-79. (Also in *Law Library Journal* 69 (Fall 1976): 100-101.)

> Statement lists specific responsibilities of lending libraries and reprint and microform publishers in the "spirit of disseminating the accumulated wealth of world scholarship."

C 3.7   Lynden, Frederick C. "Replacement of hard copy by microforms." *Microform Review* 4, 1 (January 1975): 15-24.

> Briefly discusses practical aspects of selection of materials for microreproduction, type of microform, binding vs. filming costs, maintenance of microforms, user reactions, equipment, bibliographic control, and other factors relevant to decision-making by librarians regarding microreproduction.

C 3.8   Darling, Pamela W. "Developing a preservation microfilming program." *Library Journal* 99 (November 1, 1974): 2803-2809. illus., bibliog.

> Administrative aspects of microfilming as a preservation technique. Discusses costs, organization, policies, in-house filming vs. outside filming, locating microforms, preparation of materials, and cooperation.

C 3.9   Salmon, Stephen R. "User resistance to microforms in the research library." *Microform Review* 3, 3 (July 1974): 194-99. bibliog.

Discusses users' attitudes toward use of microforms, identifying sources of complaints and suggesting ways of coping with the difficulties of bibliographical control, equipment defects, and "human interface."

C 3.10   "Standards for reprint publishing; recommendations for control of editorial quality." *Special Libraries* 63, 7 (July 1972): 359. (Report of the Rare Book Libraries Conference on Facsimiles.)

Editorial standards for microfilm and hard copy facsimiles.

C 3.11   Lane, Alfred H. "Reprints in the preservation picture, and a drift aside." *Special Libraries* 63, 7 (July 1972): 305-09.

Briefly discusses the reprint industry, problems, pricing, standards and controls, and library responsibilities, in the context of reprinting as a preservation technique.

C 3.12   Sajor, Ladd E. "Preservation microfilming: why, what, when, who, how." *Special Libraries* 63, 4 (April 1972): 195-201.

Discusses choosing materials for microfilming and executing a microfilm program.

C 3.13   Hawken, William R. *Copying Methods Manual.* Chicago: American Library Association, 1966. 375 pp., illus., bibliog., glossary. (Library Technology Program Publication No. 11)

Deals with the processes, methods, techniques, and equipment used for reproducing documents. Includes schematics and tables outlining the processes and standards. Includes annotated bibliography.

C 4 Equipment

C 4.1 "Photocopying equipment." *Library Technology Reports,* 1965-

Descriptions of photocopy processes, image quality, characteristics of machine types, administrative aspects, costs, and availability. Reports on equipment include specifications, special features, maintenance, costs, test observations, and general appraisal. Cumulative table of contents is updated annually.

C 4.2 Saffady, William. "Evaluating coin-operated copying equipment for library applications." *Library Resources and Technical Services* 20, 2 (Spring 1976): 115-22.

Develops a policy for the organization of a coin-operated copier program. Considerations in the selection of machines including machine evaluation, supply and service requirements, pricing plans, maintenance contracts, and patron use.

C 4.3 Saffady, William. "New developments in electrostatic copiers." *American Archivist* 38, 1 (January 1975): 67-75. (Technical notes)

Discusses full-size document reproduction of "hard-to-copy" originals. Important features of copiers, brand name copiers, requirements for copying in archives, paper stocks, technical requirements, and costs.

C 4.4 Ballou, Hubbard W., ed. *Guide to Microreproduction Equipment.* Silver Springs, Maryland: National Microfilm Association, 1971. 5th ed. 793 pp.

Guide to cameras, readers, reader/printers, processors, duplicators, enlargers, and accessories including manufacturers, distributors, model names, specifications, dimensions, special features, accessories, and prices. Annual supplement published.

Part I

D

Conservation Techniques

D 1   General Repair Techniques

D 1.1   Brown, Margaret, Donald Etherington, and Linda McWilliams. *Design and Construction of Boxes for the Protection of Rare Books.* Washington, D. C.: Library of Congress, forthcoming.

> Instructions for making boxes for rare books including specifications, construction procedures, diagrams, and materials for a phased preservation box, lip-on casing box, and portfolio. Compiled in the Preservation Office of the Library of Congress.

D 1.2   Poole, Frazer G. "The physical protection of brittle and deteriorating documents." *Library Scene* 5, 2 (June 1976): 9-11.

> Description of lamination and encapsulation techniques used at the Library of Congress, including rationale for selection of technique, materials, suppliers, and encapsulation instructions.

D 1.3   Poole, Frazer G. "Current lamination policies of the Library of Congress." *American Archivist* 39, 2 (April 1976): 157-59.

> Recommends polyester encapsulation over Barrow lamination for "documents which will be preserved indefinitely as distinguished from those which need to be preserved 50-75 years or less." Precise policy statement on a foggy issue.

D 1.4   Banks, Paul N. "The conservation of maps and atlases." *AB Bookman's Yearbook, Part 1* (1976): 53-63.

> General article on conservation with special mention of maps. Includes environmental control, protective storage, treatment, and mention of the development of the field of library and archives conservation.

D 1.5   Burdett, Eric. "Repairs to books." In *The Craft of Bookbinding: a Practical Handbook* (London: David and Charles, 1975), pp. 331-47. illus.

Repairs to cloth casings including cleaning covers and book edges, new endpapers, plates and maps, recasing and reinforcing cover spines, new spines, and corners. Repairs to leather bindings including relacing boards, rebacking, mounting original spines, and tightback repairs.

D 1.6 Cains, Anthony. "New attitudes to conservation." In Philip Smith, *New Directions in Bookbinding* (New York: Van Nostrand Reinhold, 1974), pp. 164-72.

Definition of the terms, techniques, and major principles of restoration and conservation with an emphasis on "honesty" in methods, materials, and documentation of treatments. Includes collation, image fixing, washing, bleaching, sizing, deacidification, buffering, mending, binding, and boxing.

D 1.7 Greenfield, Mary E. "Mylar envelopes." *Guild of Book Workers Journal* 11, 3 (1973): 23-27. illus.

Detailed, illustrated instructions for polyester encapsulation using "Mylar."

D 1.8 Tribolet, Harold W. "Rare book and paper repair techniques." *History News* 25, 3 (March 1970). (AASLH technical leaflet 13)

Discursive approach to the repair of rare paper and books. Background and philosophy of restoration.

D 1.9 Banks, Paul N. "Paper cleaning." *Restaurator* 1 (1969): 52-66.

Description of dry, solvent, and wet cleaning methods for paper. Includes mention of methods recommended by specific individuals.

D 1.10 Horton, Carolyn. *Cleaning and Preserving Bindings and Related Materials.* Chicago: American Library Association, 1969. 2d ed. (Library Technology Program Publication No. 16) 87 pp., illus.

Specific procedures and techniques in the reconditioning, repair and protection of library materials. Appendices list supplies, sources, and equipment.

D 2 *Leather Bookbindings*

D 2.1   Library of Congress. *Preserving Leather Bookbindings.* Washington, D. C.: Library of Congress, 1975. (Preservation Leaflet Series, no. 3.) 4 pp.

> Explanation of acid deterioration of leather, standards for optimum storage conditions, and methods of cleaning and treatment of bindings. Includes formulas and sources.

D 2.2   Banks, Paul N. *Treating Leather Bookbindings.* Chicago: The Newberry Library, 1974. Rev. ed. 4 pp.

> Discussion of chemical and physical deterioration of bookbinding leather and treatments.

D 2.3   Elliott, Roy G. H. "Leather as a bookbinding material." *Designer Bookbinders Review*   2 (Autumn 1973): 2-8; 3 (Spring 1974): 11-16; 4 (Autumn 1974): 11-15.

> Three part article discusses historical background of leather as a bookbinding material, manufacturing processes, and deterioration and durability.

D 2.4   Middleton, Bernard. *The Restoration of Leather Bindings.* Chicago: American Library Association, 1972. (Library Technology Program Publication No. 18.) 201 pp., illus., bibliog.

> Detailed procedures for restoring leather bookbindings. Includes definitions of terms, tools, equipment, and materials.

D 3   Bookbinding and Case Histories

D 3.1   Frost, Gary. "Conservation standard rebinding of single books: a review of current practice at the Newberry Library." *AIC Preprints* (1977): 56-61. (Paper presented at the 5th annual meeting of the American Institute for Conservation of Historic and Artistic Works)

> Presents a philosophy for the rebinding of a seventeenth century printed book which was poorly rebound in the nineteenth century as a prototype in the development of conservation rebinding techniques. Outlines steps and techniques, and the principles behind them. Highlights crucial areas and conflicts.

D 3.2   Cains, Anthony. "Techniques of preservation based on early binding methods and materials." *The Paper Conservator* 1 (1976): 2-8.

> Specifications for rebinding structure, techniques, and materials based on the examination of hundreds of examples from the Biblioteca Nazionale Centrale, Florence, and Trinity College. Development of experimental models. Includes specifications for re-using all or part of the original; new covers and binding; bookmaking; and a sequence of operations for the repair of early printed books.

D 3.3   Pollard, Graham. "On the repair of medieval bindings." *The Paper Conservator* 1 (1976): 35-36.

> Lists general principles in the repair of a medieval binding including documentation, specifications, agreements between librarian and bookbinder, requirements for new materials, effects of structure of rebinding, disposition of fragments, and conditions of exceptions "in order that the materials for a study of medieval binding practice not be further contaminated or destroyed."

D 3.4   Powell, Roger. "Case history of repair and rebinding of an eighth century vellum manuscript." In Philip Smith,

New Directions in Bookbinding (New York: Van Nostrand Reinhold, 1974), pp. 174-83.

Discussion of the rebinding operation in a philosophical framework. Includes details of original condition, collation, investigation during "take-down," documentation of work, and particulars of treatment. Photographs of two previous restorations.

D 3.5   Banks, Paul N. "The treatment of an 1855 British paper specimen book." *International Institute for Conservation of Historic and Artistic Works, Bulletin of the American Group* 12, 2 (1972): 88-95.

Historical background on the book and its paper specimens. Statement of original condition, description of subsequent treatments and new binding structure.

D 3.6   Cockerell, Douglas. *Bookbinding, and the Care of Books; A Text-Book for Bookbinders and Librarians.* London: Sir Isaac Pitman and Sons, 1971. 5th ed., rev. 345 pp., illus. (Originally published in 1962.)

Standard source for a philosophy of book conservation, including description of the best methods and materials and the rationales behind them.

D 3.7   Banks, Paul N. "The treatment of the first edition of Melville's *The Whale.*" In International Institute for Conservation of Historic and Artistic Works, American Group, *Technical Papers from 1968 through 1970* (New York: IIC-AG, 1970), pp. 175-80.

Advocates case histories of book restorations. Description of treatment and rebinding including methods, materials, and reasons behind decisions.

D 3.8   Tribolet, Harold W. "Binding practice as related to the preservation of books." *Library Quarterly* 40, 1 (January 1970): 128-37. bibliog.

Brief description of the evolution in binding structures, structural elements that must be considered in rebinding, variations in methods of sewing, and characteristic types of binding.

Lists components of three types of rebinding, for "books of permanent interest, but of no special value," for "rare or valuable books," and "simple rebinding." Discusses decline in quality of materials and techniques.

D 3.9   Lehmann-Haupt, Hellmut.   "On the rebinding of old books." In *Bookbinding in America: Three Essays* (New York: R. R. Bowker, 1967). Rev. ed. (Originally published in 1941.)

Philosophical discussion of rebinding of old books. Introduces the idea of a "conservation" rebinding, where permanent materials and methods are more important than the "fineness" of the work.

D 4 Commercial Library Binding

D 4.1   Tanselle, G. Thomas. "Bibliographers and the library." *Library Trends* 25 (April 1977): 745-62.

> Emphasizes the importance of "physical evidence" to the bibliographer. Discusses the implications of rebinding, the importance of the original binding and dust jacket, and summarizes the bibliographers point of view as distinct from that of the average librarian. Advocates respect for books as physical objects.

D 4.2   Farkas, Andrew. "Random thoughts on binding, binderies, librarians, library schools and other related matters." *Library Scene* 5, 2 (June 1976): 14-17.

> Discusses the absence in library school curricula of training in binding skills, familiarity with bindery practices, and evaluation of library binders. "What librarians ought to know about library binding."

D 4.3   Tauber, Maurice F., ed. *Library Binding Manual: A Handbook of Useful Procedures for the Maintenance of Library Volumes.* Boston: Library Binding Institute, 1972. 185 pp., glossary.

> Designed as an introduction to commercial library binding practices, to assist librarians in preparation of materials prior to binding. Includes the Library Binding Institute Standards for library binding. Useful as instruction on how commercial binderies operate, not necessarily how they should operate.

D 4.4   Roberts, Matt. "The role of the librarian in the binding process." *Special Libraries* 62 (October 1971): 413-20.

> Describes the fundamentals of commercial binding as a guide to librarians in exercising control over the quality of binding. Lists aspects to be included in specifications and criteria for sending books for commercial binding.

D 4.5   Henderson, William T. "Binding—a librarian's view." In Walter C. Allen, ed. *Serial Publication in Large Libraries* (Urbana: University of Illinois Graduate School of Library   Science, 1970), pp. 95-107.   bibliog. (Allerton Park Institute, no. 16)

> Librarianship's rationale for the commercial binding of serials. Administrative and organizational aspects, and binding standards. Mention of preservation problems.

D 4.6   Roberts, Matt.   "Oversewing and the problem of book preservation in the research library." *College and Research Libraries* 28 (January 1967): 17-24.

> Critical discussion of "oversewing" as employed by mass production commercial binderies and mention of alternative methods. Economic forces that have led to the decline of binding standards, binding and preservation problems of research libraries, and responsibility of librarians for binding quality.

D 5.1   Kelly, George B., and John C. Williams. "Mass deacidification with diethyl zinc, large-scale trials." *AIC Preprints* (1978): 81-92. (Paper presented at the 6th annual meeting of the American Institute for Conservation of Historic and Artistic Works). illus.

Describes a LC experiment with mass deacidification using diethyl zinc vapor under pressure as the deacidification agent. The experiment determined the best operating procedures and estimates of the cost of treatment. The process took eight days and appears feasible on a commercial scale.

D 5.2   Kelly, George B., Lucia C. Tang, and Marta K. Krasnow. "Methylmagnesium carbonate—an improved non-aqueous deacidification agent." In Williams, John C., ed., *Preservation of Paper and Textiles of Historical and Artistic Value* (Washington, D. C.: American Chemical Society, 1977), pp. 62-71. (Advances in Chemistry Series, no. 164)

Compares methylmagnesium carbonate (prepared by carbonation of a solution of magnesium methoxide) with magnesium methoxide as a deacidification agent. Recommends methylmagnesium carbonate as being a superior agent—developed at the Preservation Research and Testing Laboratory of the Library of Congress.

D 5.3   Smith, Richard D. "Design of a liquified gas mass deacidification system for paper and books." In Williams, John C., ed., *Preservation of Paper and Textiles of Historical and Artistic Value* (Washington, D. C.: American Chemical Society, 1977), pp. 149-58. illus. (Advances in Chemistry Series, no. 164)

Describes the Wei T'o Non-aqueous Book Deacidificiation System, an in-progress pilot project at the Public Archives of Canada, including institutional background, system selection, characteristics of liquified gas systems, and current system design.

D 5.4   Smith, Richard D. "Paper deacidification, part 3 and 4."
         Art Dealer and Framer (November 1976): 40-46;
         (December 1976): 7-12.

         Concepts underlying nonaqueous deacidification, discussion of
         Wei T'o solution, guidelines for recommending deacidification
         to clients, details of treatment, and precautions.

D 5.5   Jonson, Lawrence F. "Preservation of art for the art
         dealer and framer, part 1; Paper deacidification,
         part 2." *Art Dealer and Framer* (August 1976): 14-15;
         (October 1976): 9-13. illus.

         Background of the process of deacidification and illustration
         of the use of Wei T'o, a commercial deacidification solution.

D 5.6   Barrow,   Restoration Shop, Inc. "The Barrow two-bath
         deacidification method." *American Archivist*   39, 2
         (April 1976): 161-64.

         Elucidation of the preparation and use of the Barrow method
         of aqueous deacidification using calcium hydroxide and calcium
         bicarbonate. Detailed formula specifications.

D 5.7   Smith, Richard D. "The deacidification of paper and
         books." *American Libraries* 6 (February 1975): 108-
         110. bibliog.

         Explanation of acid degradation of paper, deacidification,
         alkaline buffering. Mention of aqueous, non-aqueous, and
         gaseous deacidification treatments. Description of the commer-
         cially available deacidification solution, "Wei T'o," developed
         by the author.

D 5.8   Smith, Richard D. "Paper deacidification: a preliminary
         report." *Library Quarterly* 36, 4 (October 1966):
         273-92. bibliog.

         Sketches the mechanism of acid-catalyzed hydrolysis of cel-
         lulose in paper fibers. Proposes an approach to practical de-
         acidification treatments in libraries. Describes some experiments
         in deacidification.

D 6.1   Weinstein, Robert A., and Larry Booth. *Collection, Care, and Use of Historical Photographs.* Nashville: American Association for State and Local History, 1977. 222 pp., illus., bibliog.

"Part Two: How to care for historical photographs: some techniques and procedures" includes general information on preservation—storage and handling, mounting, and copies; restoration—chemical, early photographic materials, glass plates, and printing paper; and modern B/W and color photographic processes.

D 6.2   Gear, James L., Robert H. MacClaren, and Mary McKiel. "Film recovery of some deteriorated black and white negatives." *American Archivist* 40, 3 (July 1977): 363-68. (Technical notes.) illus.

Report of original condition of the deteriorated negatives and subsequent treatment. Outline of procedures, equipment, and materials.

D 6.3   Klein, Henry. "Microfilm resuscitation: a case study." *Journal of Micrographics* 9, 6 (July-August 1976): 299-303.

Description of reclamation process for water soaked reels of microfilm that had been allowed to dry.

D 6.4   Ostroff, Eugene. *Conserving and Restoring Photographic Collections.* Washington, D. C.: American Association of Museums, 1976. First published in *Museum News* 52, 8 (1974): 42-45; 53, 1 (1974): 40-42, 48; 53, 3 (1974): 42-45; 53, 4 (1974): 34-36.

Environmental contamination, temperature and relative humidity, effects of residual chemicals, processing, reprocessing, formulas for test solutions, fixer, washes, and other solutions for specific problems, restoration-optical procedures, cleaning, chemical intensification, protective coatings, storage-hazards of acid migration and adhesives, containers and display.

D 6.5   Mehra, C. P.   "Conservation of photographic archives." *Conservation of Cultural Property in India* 6 (1973): 64-76. bibliog.

Discusses the problems of deterioration in photographic archives, including preventative measures, processing, storage, handling, inspection, restoration, tests for residual hypo, and techniques for removal of residual hypo.

D 6.6   Welch, Walter L.   "Preservation and restoration of authenticity in sound recordings." *Library Trends* 21 (July 1972): 83-100.

Reviews "the state of the art of preservation and restoration of authenticity in sound recordings." Discusses criteria of quality of sound recordings, archival permanence of recordings, and current audio technology.

D 6.7   Hall, D.   "Phonorecord preservation; notes of a pragmatist." *Special Libraries* 62 (September 1971): 357-62.

Reviews basics of phonorecord preservation including storage and shelving, handling and use, supplies, and tape-copying.

D 6.8   East Street Gallery. *Procedures for Processing and Storing Black and White Photographs for Maximum Possible Permanence.*   Grinnell, Iowa: East Streeet Gallery, 1970. 44 pp., illus., bibliog.

Detailed procedures for "archival processing," including discussion of photographic paper; exposure; baths; toning; washing; hypo elimination; print mounting, framing and storage; and use of East Street Gallery products. Publication is out of print and will be superseded. *Preservation of Contemporary Photographic Materials* by Henry Willhelm (forthcoming).

D 6.9   Koefod, Curtis F.   "The handling and storage of computer tapes." *Data Processing Magazine* 11 (July 1969): 20-23, 26-28.

Discusses handling, storage, and cleaning of magnetic computer tapes; factors relating to winding equipment and shipping; damage caused by fingerprints, stray magnetism, high temperatures (including fire), and humidity.

D 6.10 Wagner, Robert W. "Motion picture restoration." *American Archivist* 32 (April 1969): 125-32. illus.

Techniques for duplicating deteriorated cellulose nitrate film and discussion of major film preservation programs in institutions.

D 6.11 Shapley, Bruce. "The care and storage of magnetic tape." *Data Processing Magazine* 10 (April 1968): 80-81.

Emphasizes control of environment, effects of fluctuating temperatures and humidity, and proper handling.

Part I

E

General Works

E 1 Bibliographies

E 1.1   "Writings on archives, historical manuscripts, and current records." Compiled in *American Archivist* 40 (April 1977): 207-33 by Elizabeth T. Edelglass, Sara C. Strom, and Sylvie J. Turner.

Annual classified bibliographies appearing one to two years after the date of publication of the citations. Pertinent sections include "Preservation and Restoration," "Buildings and Storage Equipment," and "Reproduction."

E 1.2   Strassberg, Richard. *Disaster Prevention and Control: A Select Bibliography.* Ithaca, New York: Cornell University Libraries, 1977. 2 pp.

Includes citations of bibliographies and works dealing with prevention, salvage, and restoration.

E 1.3   Rath, Frederick L. and Merrilyn R. O'Connell, eds. *A Bibliography on Historical Organization Practices: Volume 2, Care and Conservation of Collections.* Nashville: American Association for State and Local History, 1977. 107 pp.

Bibliography on the care of museum collections, including a section on library materials. Also contains an annotated "Basic Reference Shelf" and citations on environmental factors. Appendix cites periodicals.

E 1.4   Banks, Paul N. *A Selective Bibliography of Materials in English on the Conservation of Research Library Materials.* Chicago: The Newberry Library, 1978.

Classified bibliography. Format designed to acquaint readers with the field of library conservation, the literature, general principles, book materials, causes of deterioration, environmental controls, and treatments.

E 1.5   Clapp, Ann. *Reading List for Students in Conservation of Historic and Artistic Works on Paper.* Washington, D. C.: American Institute for Conservation of Historic and Artistic Works, 1976.

> Classified bibliography covering paper artifacts (chemistry, manufacture, history, conservation, and restoration) including books. Citations are coded as "required reading," "books and articles to scan," and "reference books."

E 1.6   Evans, Frank B., comp. *Modern Archives and Manuscripts: A Select Bibliography.* Washington, D. C.: Society of American Archivists, 1975. Rev. ed.

> Includes early articles. Abbreviated citations in text form. Pertinent sections include "Preservation: Buildings and Storage Facilities," and "Preservation: Repair and Restoration."

E 1.7   Cunha, George M. and Dorothy G. Cunha. *Conservation of Library Materials: A Manual and Bibliography on the Care, Repair, and Restoration of Library Materials.* Volume II: Bibliography. Metuchen, N. J.: Scarecrow, 1972. 2d ed. 414 pp.

> Classified retrospective bibliography partially annotated. Includes general references and an author index.

E 2   Serials

E 2.1   *American Archivist.* Vol. 1, 1938- . Society of American Archivists, Box 8198, University of Illinois at Chicago Circle, Chicago, Illinois 60680. Quarterly.

Occasional articles on conservation. Since 1962, the "Technical Notes" section, edited by Clark Nelson, has supplied current information on products, techniques, publications, education, research, and organizations, in the fields of reproduction, preservation, exhibits, information storage and retrieval, and buildings and equipment.

E 2.2   *Art and Archaeology Technical Abstracts.* Vol. 1, 1955- . Institute of Fine Arts, New York University, New York, for The International Institute for Conservation of Historic and Artistic Works, London. (Vols. 1-5 published as *IIC Abstracts.*)

Abstracts articles and books, primarily concerning museums and museum work. Sections concerning books and libraries. Includes indexes to authors, subjects. Classified arrangement.

E 2.3   *Bollettino dell'Istituto di Patologia del Libro.* Vol. 1, 1938- . Istituto di Patologia del Libro, Via dei Gracchi, 183, 00192 Roma, Italia.

Devoted to conservation of books and manuscripts. English summaries of non-English articles usually given. Includes news, notices, conference reports.

E 2.4   *Journal of the American Institute for Conservation.* Vol. 1, 1960-. American Institute for Conservation of Historic and Artistic Works, 1522 K Street, N.W., Washington, D.C. 20005. Biannual. (Formerly the *AIC Bulletin*).

Publishes "original contributions to treatment and research" in the theory and practice of conservation of cultural property. AIC also publishes preprints of articles presented at annual meetings.

E 2.5   *Journal of Micrographics.* Vol. 1, 1967- . National Micro-
         Association, Silver Spring, Maryland 20910. Bi-
         monthly. (Formerly *NMA Journal*.)

>   Articles on micrographics and applications to business, industry,
>   and libraries.

E 2.6   *Library Resources and Technical Services.* Vol. 1, 1957- .
         Resources and Technical Services Division, American
         Library Association, 50 East Huron Street, Chicago,
         Illinois 60611. Quarterly.

>   Occasional articles on conservation.

E 2.7   *The Library Scene.* Vol. 1, 1972- . 322 Stuart St., Bos-
         ton, Massachusetts 02116. Published by The Library
         Binding Institute. Quarterly. (Successor to *The Li-
         brary Binder*.)

>   Periodical of the commercial library binding industry.

E 2.8   *Library Technology Reports.* Vol. 1, 1965- . American
         Library Association, 50 East Huron Street, Chicago,
         Illinois 60611. Bimonthly.

>   Technical reports and evaluations of equipment, supplies,
>   materials, and systems.

E 2.9   *Microform Review.* Vol. 1, 1972- . Microform Review,
         Inc., Westport, Connecticut. Quarterly.

>   News and articles on microforms and developments in micro-
>   form technology. Reviews of micropublications.

E 2.10   *National Preservation Newsletter.* Vol. 1, 1979- . Library
         of Congress, Washington, D.C. 20540. Tri-annual.

>   Contains information about the LC Preservation Office and the
>   National Preservation Program.

E 2.11   *Paper Conservator.* Vol. 1, 1976- . Institute of Paper
         Conservation, P.O. Box 17, London WC1N 2PE,
         England. Annual.

Articles dealing with the conservation and restoration of prints and drawings and library and archival materials. Includes book reviews, supplies, information, correspondence, and calender of events. Concerned with the conservator both as a craftsman and scientist. The Institute also publishes a newsletter, *Paper Conservation News* in March, June, and September to disseminate topical news and short reports on techniques, supplies, and equipment.

E 2.12   *Restaurator.* Vol. 1, 1969- . Munksgaard International Publishers Ltd., 35 Nörre Sögade, DI-1370, Copenhagen, Denmark. Quarterly.

International journal for the preservation of library and archival material.

E 2.13   *Studies in Conservation.* Vol. 1, 1952- . The International Institute for Conservation of Historic and Artistic Works, 608 Grand Building, Trafalgar Square, London WC2, United Kingdom. Quarterly.

International journal of the museum conservation profession.

E 2.14   *Conservation Administration Newsletter.* Vol. 1, 1979- . Robert H. Patterson, Editor, P.O. Box 3334, University Station, Laramie, Wyoming 82071.

Current awareness newsletter directed towards the administrator of conservation programs.

E 2.15   *Abbey Newsletter.* Vol. 1, 1975- . 5410 85th Ave., Apt. 2, New Carrollton, Maryland 20784. Six per year.

News and conservation/binding techniques, history of bookbinding, people, programs, supplies, and literature—directed at the bookbinder concerned with conservation.

E 3 Manuals and Texts

E 3.1 Williams, John C., ed., *Preservation of Paper and Textiles of Historic and Artistic Value*. Washington, D. C.: American Chemical Society, 1977. 403 pp. (Advances in Chemistry Series, no. 164)

Articles on the care and preservation of books, manuscripts, and textiles, including paper permanence, the chemistry of paper deterioration and deacidification, techniques for the reclamation of water damaged books, and technical procedures for determining permanence.

E 3.2 Duckett, Kenneth W. *Modern Manuscripts; A Practical Manual for Their Management, Care, and Use*. Nashville: American Association for State and Local History, 1975. 375 pp., illus., bibliog.

Chapter 4, "Physical Care and Conservation," covers proper storage, environmental controls, fire and water slavage, and simple repairs. Also includes an historical treatment of more sophisticated techniques.

E 3.3 Lewis, Ralph H. *Manual for Museums*. Washington, D. C.: Department of the Interior, National Park Service, 1976. 412 pp.

Chapter 4, "Caring for the Collections," covers agents of deterioration, climatic control, study-collection space, and specimen-storage equipment. Considers preservation of exhibits.

E 3.4 Timmons, Sharon, ed. *Preservation and Conservation: Principles and Practices*. Washington, D. C.: National Trust for Historic Preservation in the U. S., Preservation Press, 1976. (Proceedings of the North American International Regional Conference, Williamsburg, Virginia and Philadelphia, September 10-16, 1972.)

Conference papers with commentaries on topics of mutual

interest to practitioners in the conservation and preservation fields. Topics include occupations and organizations; materials and techniques; standards-philosophy, procedures and performance, and accreditation/licensing; and education and range from technical discussions to development of philosophical frameworks for the field in general.

E 3.5   Kathpalia, Yash Pal. *Conservation and Restoration of Archive Materials.* Paris: UNESCO, 1973. (Documentation, Libraries, and Archives: Studies and Research, no. 3.) 231 pp.

Textbook of document preservation. Includes constituent materials and their history, causes and control of deterioration, principles of repair, techniques, short chapter on workrooms and supplies, preservation of microfilms and sound recordings. Appendices list tests, formulas, equipment, and "norms of output" (one person per day).

E 3.6   Library Association. Research and Development Committee. *The Care of Books and Documents.* London: Library Association, 1972. (Library Association Research Publication, no. 10) 23 pp., bibliog.

Covers the "enemies" of books, environment (storage, access, fire, and theft), exhibits, binding, and supply sources.

E 3.7   Cunha, George Martin, and Dorothy Grant Cunha. *Conservation of Library Materials; A Manual and Bibliography on the Care, Repair and Restoration of Library Materials.* Metuchen, N.J.: Scarecrow, 1971. 2d ed. 406 pp., illus.

Historical background, the nature of library materials, the enemies of library materials, preventative care, repair and restoration, disasters, formulas, standards, recommended practices, organizations.

E 3.8   Plenderleith, Harold James and Anthony E. A. Werner. *The Conservation of Antiquities and Works of Art: Treatment, Repair and Restoration.* London: Oxford University Press, 1971. 2d ed.

Standard reference source for the chemistry and technology of conservation and restoration.

E 3.9   Organ, Robert M. *Design for Scientific Conservation of Antiquities*. Washington, D. C.: Smithsonian Institution Press, 1968. 497 pp. illus.

> Describes the functions of a museum conservation department; analyzes the problems of design for equipment and work space for conservation processes; includes processes involved in treatment of antiquities, examples of layouts, and notes on equipment. Useful for anyone attempting to design a conservation facility.

E 3.10   Kane, Lucile M. *A Guide to the Care and Administration of Manuscripts.* Nashville: American Association for State and Local History, 1966. Rev. 2d ed.

> Chapter on "Preservation" includes simple techniques for the physical care of manuscripts.

E 4.1   Stuhrke, Richard A. "The development of permanent paper." In Williams, John C., ed., *Preservation of Paper and Textiles of Historical and Artistic Value* (Washington, D. C.: American Chemical Society, 1977), pp. 24-36. (Advances in Chemistry Series, no. 164)

Defines "paper permanence" and discusses the factors which affect the permanency and durability of paper including the components, manufacturing process, and storage conditions. Mentions research and historical background.

E 4.2   Barrow, W. J., Research Laboratory. *Permanence/Durability of the Book*. Richmond, Virginia: W. J. Barrow Research Laboratory, 1963-74. 7 vols.

Covers research projects of the Barrow Research Laboratory, funded by the Council on Library Resources. Titles of volumes are:
Vol. 1   *A Two-Year Research Program.* 1963.
Vol. 2   *Test Data of Naturally Aged Papers.* 1964.
Vol. 3   *Spray Deacidification.* 1964.
Vol. 4   *Polyvinyl Acetate (PVA) Adhesives for Use in Library Binding.* 1965.
Vol. 5   *Strength and Other Characteristics of Book Papers, 1800–1899.* 1967.
Vol. 6   *Spot Testing for Unstable Modern Book and Record Papers.* 1969.
Vol. 7   *Physical and Chemical Properties of Book Papers, 1509–1949.* 1974.

E 4.3   Barrow, William J. *Manuscripts and Documents: Their Deterioration and Restoration.* Charlottesville: University Press of Virginia, 1972. 2d ed. 84 pp., bibliog.

Reports data from laboratory studies determining the causes of the deterioration of documents and development of restorative procedures. Includes ink, paper, storage conditions, deacidification, and lamination. Second edition contains a forward by Frazer Poole on the life and work of William J. Barrow.

E 4.4   Clapp, Verner W. *Story of Permanent/Durable Book Paper, 1115–1970.* Copenhagen: Restaurator Press, 1972. (*Restaurator Supplement*, no. 3.) 51 pp. (Also appeared in *Scholarly Publishing* 2 (January 1971): 107-124; (April 1971): 229-45; (July 1971): 353-67.

> Discusses the history of book paper and its "progressive degradation since 1500 to the nineteenth century." Acidity as an agent of deterioration, and the development of specifications for and manufacture of permanent/durable book paper.

E 4.5   Smith, Richard D. *A Comparison of Paper in Identical Copies of Books from the Lawrence University, the Newberry, and the New York Public Libraries.* Copenhagen: Restaurator Press, 1972. (*Restaurator Supplement*, no. 2.) 76 pp.

> Results of a study to test the acidity in identical copies of books from three libraries in diverse locations. Confirmed the rapid deterioration of books published between 1900 and 1960. Related storage practices and urban environments to the condition of the books.

E 5.1   Banks, Paul N. "Preservation of library materials." In Kent, A., H. Lancour, and J. E. Daily, eds., *Encyclopedia of Library and Information Science*, vol. 23 (New York: Marcel Dekker, 1978), pp. 180-222. illus., bibliog.

Overview including categories of preservation, preservation methods—especially environmental control and handling and storage practices, physical treatment methods—paper treatment and bookbinding, preservation personnel and organizations, literature and standards, and preservation microfilming and cooperative programs. By its appearance in a major publication of the library profession, this article attests to the growing acceptance of preservation/conservation as a necessary library function.

E 5.2   Spawn, Willman. "Physical care of books and manuscripts." In Peters, Jean, ed., *Book Collecting: a Modern Guide* (New York: Bowker, 1977), pp. 136-58. bibliog., illus.

Succinct advice to the collector intending to preserve a collection for the future. Discusses the "most conservation for the most books with the funds on hand" including environment, storage, and protective encasement. Mentions the "specific topics" of acidity, binding, cleaning, dust jackets, exhibition, fashions and gadgets (in conservation), and assistance.

E 5.3   Cunha, George M. "Conservation and preservation of archives." Paper presented at the SAA/NEH Conference on Priorities for Funding, Chicago, Jan., 1977. Summarized with discussion in *American Archivist* 40, 3 (July 1977): 321-24.

Maintains that many conservation problems could be resolved by archivists and curators pooling resources and skills in the present, instead of waiting for conservators to provide all the answers and the means for inexpensive mass treatment. Discusses the feasibility of regional conservation facilities.

E 5.4   Poole, Frazer G. "Some aspects of the conservation problem in archives." Paper presented at the SAA/NEH Conference on Priorities for Funding, Chicago, January, 1977. Published in *American Archivist* 40, 2 (April 1977): 163-71. Summarized with discussion in *American Archivist* 40, 3 (July 1977): 321-24.

Discussion of the major problems and their extent, causes of paper deterioration, fundamentals of preservation, and innovations in conservation techniques. Recommends further research, and the initiation of training programs and briefly describes a proposed National Preservation Program.

E 5.5   Poole, Frazer G. "Preservation." In Robert L. Clark, ed. *Archives—Library Relations* (New York: R. R. Bowker, 1976), pp. 141-54.

Outlines major aspects of the preservation problem including the nature of the materials, their deterioration, conservation alternatives and directions, and sources.

E 5.6   Doms, Keith, ed. "Preservation of library materials." *PLA* (Pennsylvania Library Association) *Bulletin* 28 (November 1973): 219-51.

Issue devoted to preservation with articles on extent of the problem, cooperative conservation efforts, chemical aspects of deterioration, and water damage.

E 5.7   Wessel, Carl J. "Deterioration of library materials." In Kent, A., and H. Lancour, eds., *Encyclopedia of Library and Information Science*, vol. 7 (New York: Marcel Dekker, 1972), pp. 69-120. illus., bibliog.

Historical background of deterioration; environmental factors—effect of light, humidity, heat, and air pollution; biological agents; and acidic components in library materials. Detailed and with many references to previous research.

E 5.8   Winger, Howard W. and Richard D. Smith, eds. *Deteriora-tion and Preservation of Library Materials: the Thirty-fourth Annual Conference of the Graduate Library School; August 4-6, 1969.* Chicago: University of Chicago Press, 1970. (Originally published in *Library Quarterly*, January 1970) 200 pp.

Collection of conference papers intended to cover scholarly needs for preservation, the nature of the materials, preservation techniques, and policy and programs for preservation.

E 5.9   Banks, Paul N. "Some problems in book conservation." *Library Resources and Technical Services* 12 (Summer 1968): 330-38.

Introduction of the concept of books of "permanent research value" as a category deserving of preservation. Emphasizes need for non-destructive methods of binding, standards for techniques, research, and development of the profession of book conservation.

E 5.10   Tribolet, Harold. "Trends in preservation." *Library Trends* 13, 2 (1964-65): 208-214.

Discussion of preservation problems, philosophy and policy for repair and restoration, techniques and progress in the field.

E 5.11   Tauber, Maurice, ed. "Conservation of library materials." *Library Trends* 4, 3 (January 1956): 215-334.

Issue devoted to conservation problems, trends in publishing and binding that affect the permanence of library materials, and library policies and practices.

Part II

A

Abell, J. M.
See 141, Berger, R.

1   Accardo, S.
    "Damage to libraries in Tuscany and Venetia."
    Unesco Bulletin for Libraries 21 (May-June 1967):
    114-118.

2   Accardo, S.
    "Introduzione al corso di perfezionamento sul restauro
    librario" ("Introduction to an advanced course on book
    restoration").
    Bollettino dell'Istituto di Patologia del Libro 28 (July-
    December 1969): 135-44.

3   Accardo, S.
    "Restoration work on the National Central Library in
    Florence."
    Unesco Bulletin for Libraries 22 (January-February
    1968): 50-52.

4   "Acid free end sheets."
    Library Technology Reports, May 1970.
    (Paper)

5   Adams, R. G.
    "Librarians are enemies of books."
    AB Bookman's Yearbook, Part 1 (1971): 23-28.
    Reprinted from *Library Quarterly* 7 (July 1937):
    317-31.

6   Adelstein, P. Z.
    "Diazo or vesicular film?"
    Special Libraries 67 (November 1976): 5A.
    (letter)

7   Adelstein, P. Z.
     "Progress report: ANSI activities on stability of pro-
     cessed diazo and vesicular films."
     Journal of Micrographics 9 (January-February 1976):
     99.

8   Adelstein, P. Z., and J. L. McCrea.
     "Dark image stability of diazo films."
     Journal of Micrographics 11 (September-October 1977):
     5-12.
     Reprinted from *Journal of Applied Photographic
     Engineering* 3, 3 (Summer 1977).

9   Adelstein, P. Z., and J. B. Rhoads.
     "Standards."
     Journal of Applied Photographic Engineering 2, 2
     (Spring 1976): 64A.

10   "Agnes-soaked papers salvaged by freezing."
     Industry Week 174, 6 (August 7, 1972): 24.

11   Agrawal, O. P.
     "Conservation of Asian cultural objects: Asian materials
     and techniques."
     Museum (Unesco) 27, 4 (1975): 155-212.

12   Alden, J. E.
     "Reproduction vs. preservation: a reappraisal of the
     trend toward indiscriminate photoreproduction of rare
     books and manuscripts."
     Library Journal   91 (November 1, 1966): 5319-22.

13   Alderson, W. T.
     "Securing grant support: effective planning and prepara-
     tion."
     History News 27, 12 (December 1972): 269-80.
     (AASLH technical leaflet 62)

14   Alekseeva, I. M., and others.
     "Nauchnoe upravlenie fondami Gosudarstvennoi biblio-
     teki SSSR im V. I. Lenina; k itogam issledovaniia"
     ("Preservation of the book stocks of the Lenin State

Library; report on research").
Sovetskoe Biblioteckovedenie 4 (1974): 45-52.

15   Alkalaj, S.
"Chemical laboratory for hygiene, conservation and restoration of damaged written materials in the National Library Cyril and Methodius, Sofia."
Restaurator 1 (1969): 87-91.

16   Allen, R. V.
"Some problems are international; damaged and defaced books [in Russian]."
Library of Congress Information Bulletin 29 (September 3, 1970): 461-62.

17   Allen, S.
Victorian Bookbindings; A Pictorial Survey.
Chicago: University of Chicago Press, 1972.

Allen, W. C.
See 535, Henderson, W. T.

18   "Allentown college library suffers $100,000 flood loss."
Library Journal 96 (November 1, 1971): 3553-54.

19   Alonso, P. G.
"Archival map preservation and documentation."
Archives and Manuscripts 5 (November 1972): 8-13.

20   Alonso, P. G.
"Conservation and circulation in map libraries."
In Drazniowsky, R., ed., *Map Librarianship: Readings* (Metuchen, New Jersey: Scarecrow, 1975), pp. 359-63.

21   Alonso, P. G.
"Conservation and circulation in map libraries; a brief review."
Special Libraries Association, Geography and Map Division Bulletin 74 (December 1968): 15-18.

22   American Library Association. Resources and Technical
     Services Division. Resources Section. Reprinting Com-
     mittee.
     "Policy on lending to reprint and microform pub-
     lishers."
     Library Resources and Technical Services 19, (Spring
     1975): 178-9.
     Also in *Law Library Journal* 69 (Fall 1976): 100-01.
     (*See* C 3.6)

23   "American Library Association replies to BMI criticism of
     library binding standards."
     Book Production Industry 45, 4 (1969): 8, 10.

24   American Mutual Insurance Alliance.
     Handbook of Organic Industrial Solvents.
     Chicago: AMIA, 1972.
     4th ed.

25   American National Standards Institute.
     *American National Standard Efficiency Testing of Air-
     Cleaning Systems Containing Devices for the Removal
     of Particles.*
     New York: American National Standards Institute,
     1972.
     (ANSI N101.1-1972)

26   American National Standards Institute.
     *American National Standard Practice for Storage of
     Black and White Prints.*
     New York: American National Standards Institute,
     1974.
     (ANSI PH1.48-1974)

27   American National Standards Institute.
     *American National Standard Practice for Storage of
     Processed Photographic Plates.*
     New York: American National Standards Institute,
     1972.
     (ANSI PH1.45-1972)

28 "American Council of Learned Societies asks: please use more lasting paper."
    Publishers' Weekly   192   (November 6, 1967): 22.

29 American Library Association. Ad Hoc Committee on Flood Damaged Libraries.
    "Floods of June 1972: preliminary damage estimates."
    American Libraries 3 (December 1972): 1202-1204.

30 American Library Association. Insurance for Libraries Committee.
    "Report: the makings of a nationwide scandal."
    ALA Bulletin 62 (April 1968): 384-86.

31 American Library Association.   Library Technology Program.
    Development of Performance Standards for Binding Used in libraries, Phase II.
    Chicago: American Library Association, 1966.
    (Library   Technology   Program   Publication   no.   10)

32 American   Library   Association.   Library   Technology Program.
    Protecting the Library and Its Resources: A Guide to Physical Protection and Insurance; Report of a Study Conducted by Gage-Babcock and Associates, Inc.
    Chicago: American Library Association, 1963.
    (Library Technology Program Publication no. 7)

    American Library Association. Library Technology Program.
    See   527, Hawken, W. R.;   556, Horton, C.;   795, Middleton, B. C.

33 American Library Association. Resources and Technical Services Division. Committee on Preservation of Library Materials.
    Preservation Training and Information.
    Chicago: American Library Association, 1977.
    (*See* A 3.1)

34   American National Standards Institute.
     American National Standard Practice for Storage of Processed Safety Photographic Film Other Than Microfilm.
     New York: American National Standards Institute, 1972.
     (ANSI PH1.43-1971)

35   American National Standards Institute.
     American Standard Practice for Storage of Processed Silver-Gelatin Microfilm.
     New York: American National Standards Institute, 1970.
     (ANSI PH5.4-1970)

36   American National Standards Institute.
     American National Standard Specifications for Microfiches.
     New York: American National Standards Institute, 1969.
     (ANSI PH5.9-1970)

37   American National Standards Institute.
     American National Standard Specifications for Photographic Film for Archival Records, Silver-Gelatin Type on Cellulose Ester Base.
     New York: American National Standards Institute, 1973.
     (ANSI PH1.28-1973)

38   American National Standards Institute.
     American National Standard Specifications for Photographic Film for Archival Records, Silver-Gelatin Type on Polyester Base.
     New York: American National Standards Institute, 1976.
     (ANSI PH1.41-1976)

39   American National Standards Institute.
     Methods for Manual Processing of Black-and-White Photographic Paper.
     New York: American National Standards Institute, 1969.
     (ANSI PH4.29-1962, R1969)

40   American National Standards Institute.
     Methods for the Determination of Silver in Photo-
     graphic Films, Papers, Fixing Baths or Residues.
     New York: American National Standards Institute,
     1969.
     (ANSI PH4.33-1969)

41   American National Standards Institute.
     Requirements for Photographic Filing Enclosures for
     Storing Processed Photographic Film, Plates and Paper.
     New York: American National Standards Institute,
     1970.
     (ANSI PH4.20-1958, R1970)

42   American National Standards Institute. Z85 Committee.
     "American national standard for permanent and durable
     library catalog cards."
     Library Technology Reports, March 1973.
     (Supplies and miscellaneous)

43   American Society of Heating, Refrigerating, and Air-Con-
     ditioning Engineers.
     "Odor removal."
     In *ASHRAE Handbook and Product Directory, 1973*
     Systems (New York: ASHRAE, 1973), ch. 33.

44   American Society of Heating, Refrigerating, and Air-Con-
     ditioning Engineers.
     "Part IV, Libraries and Museums."
     In *ASHRAE Handbook and Product Directory, 1974*
     Applications (New York: ASHRAE, 1974), pp. 3.10-
     3.13.

45   Andreassen, J. C. L.
     "The conservation of writings on paper in Canada."
     Canadian Archivist 1, 7 (1969): 9-17.

46   Andreassen, J. C. L.
     "The Conservation of writings on paper in Canada."
     Records Management Quarterly 4 (January 1970): 15-
     18, 26.

Annan, G. L.
See 297, Crawford, H.

47   Appel, K.
"Bayerische Staatsbibliothek, Buchrestaurierung; Methoden und Ergebnisse" ("Bavarian State Library, restoration of books; methods and results").
Zeitschrift für Bibliothekswesen und Bibliographie 19, 3 (1972): 182-84.

48   Arad, A.
"Automated mass spraying of documents."
Archives et Bibliothèques de Belgique/Archief- en Bibliotheekwezen in België 46 (1975): 288-96.

49   Arad, A.
"A simple measurement of torsional rigidity of paper."
Restaurator 1 (1969): 69-77.

Arbeitstagung über die Massenrestaurierung von Wassergeschädigtem Papier, Buckeburg, 1970.
See 1000, Poschmann, B.

50   "Archives is printed on acid-free paper."
Archives 8 (October 1968): 171.

51   Ash, L. M.
"Institutional de-acquisitions: increasing sources of books, manuscripts."
AB Bookman's Weekly 59 (January 31, 1977): 587-88.

52   Ashby, P.
"On becoming microminded: an incitement to thought on the subject of microfilm in libraries."
Liaison (Library Association Record), September 1975, pp. 214-15.

Association of Canadian Map Libraries.
See 980, Pidek, J.

53   Association of Research Libraries. Office of Management
     Studies. Systems and Procedures Exchange Center.
     Kit 35, Preservation of Library Materials.
     Washington, D. C.: Association of Research Libraries,
     August 1977.

54   Association of Research Libraries. Office of Management
     Studies. Systems and Procedures Exchange Center.
     "Preservation of Library Materials."
     SPEC Flyer, no. 35 (August 1977).

55   Astbury, R. G.
     Bibliography and Book Production.
     Oxford and New York: Pergamon Press, 1967.

56   "At public archives: special portfolio designed for Napole-
     onic documents."
     *Feliciter; Newsletter of the Canadian Library Associa-
     tion* 22 (February 1976): 8.

     Atlas, S. M.
     See 747, Mark, H. F.

57   "Attivita del laboratorio di restauro" ("Activity of restora-
     tion laboratories").
     Bollettino dell'Istituto di Patologia del Libro 27 (July-
     December 1968): 226-48; 28 (July-December 1969):
     207-19.

58   "Attivita dell' Istituto di Patologia del Libro durante l'anno
     1971" ("Activities of the Institute for Book Pathology
     during 1971").
     Accademie e Biblioteche d'Italia 40 (July-October
     1972): 349-53.

59   Austin, J.
     "Care and feeding of photograph collections."
     Idaho Librarian 27 (January 1975): 3-7.

60   Avedon, D. M.
     "Microfilm generation and polarity terminology."
     Special Libraries 68 (April 1977): 141-44.
     (*See* C 2.1)

61 Avedon, D. M.
   "Microfilm permanence and archival quality: standards."
   Special Libraries 63 (December 1972): 586-88.
   Reprinted from *Journal of Micrographics* 6 (November-December 1972): 93-94.
   (*See* C 2.9)

62 Avedon, D. M., ed.
   NMA Standard Glossary of Micrographics.
   Silver Spring, Maryland: National Microfilm Association, 1971.
   5th ed.
   (*See* C 2.6)

63 Aziz, S. M.
   "Simple system for drying repaired documents."
   Unesco Bulletin for Libraries 30 (May-June 1976): 182.

B

64 Baer, N. S., N. Indictor, and A. Joel.
   "The aging behavior of impregnating agent-paper systems as used in paper conservation."
   Restaurator 2 (1975): 5-23.

65 Baer, N. S., N. Indictor, and W. H. Phelan.
   "An evaluation of adhesives for use in paper conservation."
   Guild of Book Workers Journal 10, 1 (1971): 17-35.

66 Baer, N. S., N. Indictor, and W. H. Phelan.
   "Evaluation of poly (vinyl acetate) adhesives for use in paper conservation."
   Restaurator 2 (1975): 121-37.

67   Baer, N. S., N. Indictor, and W. H. Phelan.
"Shelf life of commercial poly (vinyl acetate) emulsions for use in paper conservation."
Guild of Book Workers Journal 10, 1 (1971): 36-38.

68   Baer, N. S., N. Indictor, M. Shelley, and W. Eley.
"An evaluation of a dip-impregnation treatment for the conservation of deteriorated books."
Bulletin of the American Institute for Conservation of Historic and Artistic Works 13, 1 (1972): 37-47.

     Baer, N. S.
See 574, Indictor, N.; 601, Joel, A.; 975, Phelan, W. H.

69   Bahn, C. I.
"Map libraries; space and equipment."
In Drazniowsky, R., ed., *Map Librarianship: Readings* (Metuchen, New Jersey: Scarecrow, 1975), pp. 364-84.

70   Baillie, W. J.
"Conservator in the New Zealand research library."
New Zealand Libraries 34 (October 1971): 89-92.

71   Baker, J.
" 'Books in peril' at NY library a scary show."
Publishers' Weekly 204 (July 16, 1973): 90.

72   Baker, J.
"Conservation must not wait."
NYLA Bulletin 23 (February 1975): 1+.

73   Baker, J.
"Restoration of library materials: some administrative considerations."
Library Scene 3 (December 1974): 4-6.
(*See* A 1.4)

74   Baker, J.
"Typical costs in planning for the small library."
Library Security Newsletter 1 (November 1975): 1.

75   Baldwin, R. M.
     "The whole book, please."
     Wilson Library Bulletin 47 (1973): 800.

76   Ballou, H., ed.
     Guide of Microreproduction Equipment.
     Silver Spring, Maryland: National Microfilm Association,
     1971.
     5th ed.
     (*See* C 4.4)

77   Ballou, H., and others.
     *Guidelines for Use in Producing Facsimiles of Rare
     Books and Related Materials.*
     Washington, D. C.: C. M. Spaulding, 1972.

78   Banerjee, P. K.
     "Maintenance and verification of stock in libraries."
     Indian Librarian 25 (September 1970): 94-96.

79   Banks, P. N.
     "Books in peril; cooperative approaches to conserva-
     tion."
     Library Journal 101 (November 15, 1976): 2348-51.
     (*See* A 4.4)

80   Banks, P. N.
     "Conservation of maps and atlases."
     AB Bookman's Yearbook, Part 1 (1976): 53-63.
     (*See* D 1.4)

81   Banks, P. N.
     "Education for conservators of library and archival
     materials."
     Library Journal (in press spring 1978)

82   Banks, P. N.
     "Environmental standards for storage of books and
     manuscripts."
     Library Journal 99 (February 1, 1974): 339-43.
     (*See* B 2.5)

83   Banks, P. N.
         Lamination.
         Chicago: The Newberry Library, 1974.
         Rev. ed.

84   Banks, P. N.
         "The librarian as conservator."
         Library Quarterly 40 (January 1970): 192-98.
         (*See* A 3.4)

85   Banks, P. N.
         Matting and Framing Documents and Art Objects on Paper.
         Chicago: The Newberry Library, 1971.

86   Banks, P. N.
         "Paper cleaning."
         Restaurator 1 (1969): 52-66.
         (*See* D 1.9)

87   Banks, P. N.
         "Preservation of library materials."
         In Kent, A., H. Lancour, and J. E. Daily, eds., *Encyclopedia of Library and Information Science*, vol. 23 (New York: Marcel Dekker, 1978), pp. 180-222.
         (*See* E 5.1)

88   Banks, P. N.
         "Problems in the examination of books and manuscripts."
         In English, D. M., and J. M. English, eds., *Proceedings of the First Georgetown Conference on Surface Analysis, Washington, D. C., 1969*
         (Washington, D. C.: Georgetown University Law Center, 1970).

89   Banks, P. N.
         Professional Training in Library and Archives Conservation.
         Chicago: The Newberry Library, 1975.
         (*See* A 3.2)

90 Banks, P. N.
    Review of Y. P. Kathpalia, *Conservation and Restoration of Archive Materials.*
    Studies in Conservation 20 (February 1975): 36-39.

91 Banks, P. N.
    "The scientist, the scholar and the book conservator: some thoughts on book conservation as a profession."
    Atti Della XLIX Riumione della S.I.P.S. Siena, 23-27 Settembre, 1967 (September 1967): 1213-19.
    (*See* A 3.6)

92 Banks, P. N.
    A Selective Bibliography of Materials in English on the Conservation of Research Library Materials.
    Chicago: The Newberry Library, 1978.
    (*See* E 1.4)

93 Banks, P. N.
    "Some problems in book conservation."
    Library Resources and Technical Services 12 (Summer 1968): 330-38.
    (*See* E 5.9)

94 Banks, P. N.
    Treating Leather Bookbindings.
    Chicago: The Newberry Library, 1974.
    rev. ed.
    (*See* D 2.2)

95 Banks, P. N.
    "The treatment of an 1855 British paper specimen book."
    International Institute for Conservation of Historic and Artistic Works, Bulletin of the American Group 12, 2 (1972): 88-95.
    (*See* D 3.5)

96 Banks, P. N.
    "The treatment of the first edition of Melville's *The Whale.*"

In International Institute for Conservation of Historic and Artistic Works—American Group, *Technical Papers From 1968 Through 1970* (New York: IIC-AG, 1970), pp. 175-80.
(*See* D 3.7)

97 Bansa, H.
"Conservation and restoration workshops working for libraries."
IFLA Journal 1, 2 (1975): 210-20.

98 Barker, N.
"Biblioteca Nazionale at Florence."
Book Collector 18 (Spring 1969): 11-22.

99 Barker, N.
"Blight in Bloomsbury."
TLS 3947 (November 18, 1977): 3959.

100 Barberi, F.
"La conservazione e il restauro. ("Conservation and restoration").
Accademie e Biblioteche d'Italia 35 (November 1967): 455-61.

101 Barberi, F.
"Dal libro raro e di pregio al bene librario" ("From rare and valuable book to a good book").
Accademie e Biblioteche d'Italia 42 (May 1974): 167-81.

102 Barnett, D.
"Preservation of disc and tape recordings."
In Library Association of Australia, *1969 Conference Proceedings, Adelaide* (Library Association of Australia, 1971), pp. 419-22.

103 Barr, P.
"Book conservation and university library administration."
College and Research Libraries 7 (July 1946): 214-19.
(*See* A 1.9)

104   Barrow Research Laboratory.
       Permanence/Durability of the Book; Vol. 1: A Two
       Year Research Program.
       Richmond, Virginia: W. J. Barrow Research Laboratory,
       1963.
       (*See* E 4.2)

105   Barrow Research Laboratory.
       Permanence/Durability of the Book; Vol. 2: Test Data
       of Naturally Aged Papers.
       Richmond, Virginia: W. J. Barrow Research Laboratory,
       1964.
       (*See* E 4.2)

106   Barrow Research Laboratory.
       Permanence/Durability of the Book; Vol. 3: Spray
       Deacidification.
       Richmond, Virginia: W. J. Barrow Research Laboratory,
       1964.
       (*See* E 4.2)

107   Barrow Research Laboratory.
       Permanence/Durability of the Book; Vol. 4: Polyvinyl
       Acetate (PVA) Adhesives for Use in Library Binding.
       Richmond, Virginia: W. J. Barrow Research Laboratory,
       1965.
       (*See* E 4.2)

108   Barrow Research Laboratory.
       Permanence/Durability of the Book; Vol. 5: Strength
       and Other Characteristics of Book Papers, 1800-1899.
       Richmond, Virginia: W. J. Barrow Research Laboratory,
       1967.
       (*See* E 4.2)

109   Barrow Research Laboratory.
       Permanence/Durability of the Book; Vol. 6: Spot
       Testing for Unstable Modern Book and Record Papers.
       Richmond, Virginia: W. J. Barrow Research Laboratory,
       1969.
       (*See* E 4.2)

110   Barrow Research Laboratory.
       *Permanence/Durability of the Book; Vol. 7: Physical
       and Chemical Properties of Book Papers, 1507-1949.*
       Richmond, Virginia: W. J. Barrow Research Laboratory,
       1974.
       (*See* E 4.2)

       Barrow Research Laboratory.
          See 1277, Walker, B.

111   "Barrow research laboratory of Richmond, Virginia, has
       entered a new two-year program cycle."
       Bibliographical Society of America Papers 66 (January
       1972): 75.

112   "Barrow research to run book preservation project."
       Library Journal 101 (May 15, 1976): 1164.

113   Barrow Restoration Shop, Inc.
       "The Barrow two-bath deacidification method."
       American Archivist 39 (April 1976): 161-64.
       (*See* D 5.6)

114   Barrow, W. J.
       "Acidity: an undesirable property in paste and mending
       tissue."
       American Archivist 30 (January 1967): 190-93.

115   Barrow, W. J.
       *Manuscripts and Documents: Their Deterioration and
       Restoration.*
       Charlottesville: University Press of Virginia, 1972.
       2d ed.
       (*See* E 4.3)

116   Barrow, W. J., and A. M. Carlton.
       "Durability of three current laminating tissues."
       American Archivist 30 (July 1967): 526-29.

117   Barrow, W. J., and A. M. Carlton.
       "Permanence of laminating tissue."
       American Archivist 31 (January 1968): 88-91.

118   Barth, M.
       "Notes on conservation and restoration of photo-
       graphs."
       The Print Collectors Newsletter 7, 2 (May-June 1976):
       48-51.

119   Baryshnikova, Z. P.
       "Some observations on the development and nutrition
       of booklice."
       Restaurator 1 (1970): 199-212.

120   Basile, C.
       "A method of making papyrus and fixing and preserving
       it by means of a chemical treatment."
       In International Institute for Conservation of Historic
       and Artistic Works, *Conservation of Paintings and the
       Graphic Arts*   (London: IIC, 1972), pp. 901-905.

121   "Battle against book-rot: grant to Barrow Preservation
       Research, Inc."
       Australian Library Journal   25, 5 (June 1976): 175.

122   Baynes-Cope, A. D.
       "The dismounting of 'dry mounted' photographic
       prints."
       Restaurator 2 (1972): 1-3.

123   Baynes-Cope, A. D.
       "The effect of residues of manganese compounds in
       paper on the bleaching of prints, etc."
       The Paper Conservator 2 (1977): 3.

124   Baynes-Cope, A. D.
       "The non-aqueous deacidification of documents."
       Restaurator 1 (1969): 2-9.

125   Baynes-Cope, A. D.
       "An organic solvent for dissolving old flour paste."
       Restaurator 2 (1972): 25-27.

       Baynes-Cope, A. D.
       See 161, Bond, M. F.

126   Beatty, W. K.
      "What monstrous creature is this?"
      Journal of the American Medical Association 212, 1
      (1970): 141-43.

127   Beck, W. L.
      "A realistic approach to microform management."
      Microform Review 2 (July 1973): 172-76.

      Becker, J.
      See 529, Hayes, R. M.

      Beckman, M.
      See 680, Langmead, S.

128   Beeching, W. A.
      Century of the Typewriter.
      London: Heinemann, 1974.

129   Beecroft, G. F.
      "Computer process control in papermaking."
      Penrose Annual 67 (1974): 205-208.

130   Beeman, D. R.
      "Micrographic standards for containers (cartridge and
      cassette) for 16 mm roll microfilm."
      Journal of Micrographics 9 (November-December
      1975): 51-55.

131   Beers, R. J.
      "New fire control techniques for records storage."
      Records Management Journal 4, 3 (Autumn 1966):
      29-32.

132   "Beinecke book bugs get cold treatment."
      American Libraries 9 (January 1978): 26.

133   Belanger, T.
      "The price of preservation."
      TLS 3947 (November 18, 1977): 1358-59.
      (*See* A 2.2)

134   Belaya, I. K.
      "Instructions for the softening of parchment manu-
      scripts and bookbindings."
      Restaurator 1 (1969): 49-51.

135   Belaya, I. K.
      "Selecting and testing adhesives for the restoration of
      skin-bindings and parchments."
      Restaurator 1 (1970): 221-231.

136   Belaya, I. K.
      "Softening and restoration of parchment in manu-
      scripts and bookbindings."
      Restaurator 1 (1969): 20-48.

137   Bell, M.
      "The cost of clean air."
      Air Conditioning, Heating and Ventilation 65 (1968):
      41-46.

138   Benedon, W.
      "Features of new records center buildings."
      Records Management Quarterly 1 (January 1967):
      14-21.

      Bennett, W. E.
      See 301, Crook, D. M.

139   Bennon, B. A.
      "Book restoration in Florence."
      Publishers' Weekly 192 (November 6, 1967): 27-28.

140   Berck, B.
      "Investigation of fumigants; I: Nature and properties
      of fumigants."
      Occupational Health Review 18, 1 (1966): 16-26.

141   Berger, R., N. Evans, J. M. Abell, and M. A. Resnik.
      "Radiocarbon dating of parchment."
      Nature 235 (1975): 160-61.

142 Berkell, W.
Böckers vård och renovering.
Stockholm: Bokvannerna, 1968.

143 Bermane, D.
"On the resistance to fading of silver-dye-bleach transparencies."
In Royal Photographic Society of Great Britain, *The Conservation of Colour Photographic Records* (London: Royal Photographic Society of Great Britain, 1974).

144 Biblioteca Apostolica Vaticana.
Conservation et reproduction des manuscrits et imprimés anciens ("Conservation and reproduction of manuscripts and ancient books").
Vatican: Biblioteca Apostolica Vaticana, 1977.

145 Biblioteca Nazionale Centrale di Firenze.
Un' Esperienza di Restauro: la Cooperativa L.A.T. pev i Beni Culturali ("Experience in restoration; the Cooperative L.A.T. for the Cultural Good").
Florence: Cooperativa L.A.T., 1974.

146 Bidwell, J.
"Paper and papermaking: 100 sources."
AB Bookman's Weekly 61 (February 13, 1978): 1043-61.

147 Bird, A. J.
"Map conservation in an academic geography department."
Aslib Proceedings 26 (February 1974): 69-73.

148 "Black/white processing for permanence: notes from Kodak pamphlet no. J-19."
Special Libraries Association, Picture Division *Picturescope* 19 (Summer 1971): 97-99.

149 Blackman, G.
"Conservation of library materials at the New York Botanical Garden."
Guild of Book Workers Journal 14 (Fall 1975): 8-11.

Blackwell, R. J.
See 1152, Spuck, W. H.

150 Blades, W.
"Enemies of books."
AB Bookman's Yearbook, Part 1 (1971): 3-22.
(Abridged text from the revised edition of 1888)

151 Blair, R. N.
"The Cameron comes of age."
Book Production Industry 48, 9 (1972): 33-38.

152 Blaquière, H.
"Le microfilm dans les archives; aspects théoriques"
("Microfilm in archives; theoretical aspects").
Gazette des Archives 67 (1969): 239-54.
Abstract in *American Archivist* 33 (October 1970): 421.

Bloom, S. M.
See 1067, Rodgers, H. G.

153 Bloy, C. H.
A History of Printing Ink, Balls and Rollers, 1440-1850.
Barnet (Herts.): Wynkyn de Worde Society, 1967.

Blumenfeld, C.
See 609, Jordan, R.

154 Blunn, D.
"A method of dry repair."
Journal of the Society of Archivists 4 (October 1972):
521-22.

155 Blunn, D., and G. Petherbridge.
"Leaf-casting—the mechanical repair of paper artifacts."
The Paper Conservator 1 (1976): 26-32.

156 Boak, R. I.
"Restoration and preservation of maps."
In Drazniowsky, R., ed., *Map Librarianship: Readings*
(Metuchen, New Jersey: Scarecrow, 1975), pp. 385-88.
Reprinted from *Special Libraries Association Geography
and Map Division Bulletin* 81 (September 1970): 21-23.

157 Bobeen, J. E.
"Mutilation of library resources: containing a study of mutilation of the reference collection of the under-graduate library, Ellis Library, University of Missouri-Columbia."
Research paper, University of Missouri-Columbia, 1974.

158 Bohem, H.
"A seam-free envelope for archival storage of photographic negatives."
American Archivist 38 (July 1975): 403-405.
(Technical notes)

159 Bohem, H.
"Visible file catalog for photographic materials."
American Archivist 39 (April 1976): 165-66.

160 Bokman, W.
The Care of Photographic Colour Materials, Restoration Aspects and Archival Processing in General.
Ottawa: Canadian Conservation Institute, April 1974.
(manuscript)

161 Bond, M. F., and A. D. Baynes-Cope.
"Fungicides."
Journal of the Society of Archivists 4 (April 1970): 51-52.
(Technical notes)

162 Boni, A., ed.
Photographic Literature; An International Bibliographic Guide to the General and Specialized Literature on Photographic Processes, Techniques, Theory, Chemistry, Physics, Apparatus, Materials and Applications, Industry, History, Biography, Aesthetics.
New York: Morgan and Morgan, 1962.

163 Boni, A., ed.
Photographic Literature.
New York: Morgan and Morgan, 1972.
(1st Supplemental Volume)

164   Bonn, T. L.
       "Microfilm restoration project."
       Cornell University Libraries Bulletin 181 (January
       1973): 8-10.

165   "Book conservation program run at Columbia and Rutgers."
       Library Journal 101 (July 1976): 1472.

166   "Book conservation: working session of experts."
       Liaison (Library Association Record) December 1971,
       p. 80.

167   "Book loss, vandalism in Toronto libraries."
       *Feliciter; Newsletter of the Canadian Library Associa-
       tion* 21 (June 1975): 8-9.

168   "Book workmanship scored by Ohio librarians."
       Library Journal 100 (January 15, 1975): 84.

169   "Books in peril: a mini-symposium on the preservation of
       library materials."
       Library Journal 101 (November 15, 1976): 2341-51.

       Booth, L.
       See 1300, Weinstein, R. A.

170   Born, L. K.
       "Planning for scholarly photocopying."
       Microform Review 1 (July 1972): 181-97.
       Reprinted from *PMLA* 79, 2 (September 1964): 77-90.

171   Boucher, A.
       Le Service de Préservation et de Réparation ("Work of
       preservation and restoration").
       La Pocatière, Quebec: Stage en Bibliothéconomie,
       Collège de Saint-Anne-de-la-Pocatière, 1970.
       2d. ed. rev.
       (Collection Guides du Personnel, no. 2)

172   Bouchot, H.
       "Types, presses, and paper."
       In Grevel, H., ed., *The Book: Its Printers, Illustrators,
       and Binders, From Gutenberg to the Present Time*
       (Detroit: Gale Research Company, 1971), pp. 250-61.

173 Bouscher, H.
"Microforms: can they save our treasures?"
Journal of Micrographics 7 (January-February 1974):
119-22.

174 Boustead, W.
"Conservation techniques in relation to archives."
In Library Association of Australia, *1971 Conference
Proceedings, Sydney* (Library Association of Australia,
1972), pp. 202-209.

175 Bozza Mariani, M.
"Del restauro librario" ("On book restoration").
Accademie e Biblioteche d'Italia 40 (May, 1972):
194-202.

176 Bradley, C. J., ed.
Manual of Music Librarianship.
Ann Arbor, Michigan: Music Libraries Association,
1966.

177 Brahm, W.
"A regional approach to conservation: the New England
Document Conservation Center."
American Archivist 40 (October 1977): 421-27.
(*See* A 4.1)

178 Branchamp, R. R.
"A simple layout for the washing and bleaching of
prints and drawings."
*International Institute for Conservation of Historic and
Artistic Works, Bulletin of the American Group* 9, 1
(1968): 21-22.

179 Brawne, M.
Libraries: Architecture and Equipment.
New York: Praeger, 1970.

180 "Break for bibliophiles."
Chemical Week 98, 17 (April 23, 1966): 93-94.

181   Breed, E.
      "You can preserve books by study, teaching book care,
      preparing for disasters."
      Wisconsin Library Bulletin   72 (November-December
      1974): 273-74.

182   Breillat, P.
      "Temporary exhibitions in libraries."
      Unesco Bulletin for Libraries   21 (January-February
      1967): 2-10.

183   Brenegan, S.
      *The Conservation of Writings on Paper—A Summary
      from the Literature.*
      Montreal: McGill University Archives, 1970.
      Reprinted in *Records Management Quarterly* 5 (January
      1971): 16-20, 27.

184   Brian, C.
      "The early paper processes."
      In Royal Photographic Society of Great Britain, *The
      Recognition of Early Photographic Processes, Their
      Care and Conservation.* (London: Royal Photographic
      Society of Great Britain, 1974).

185   British Standards Institution.
      "Preservation standards."
      Liaison (Library Association Record), May 1974, p. 36.

186   British Standards Institution.
      *Recommendations for the Storage and Exhibition of
      Archival Documents.*
      London: British Standards Institution, 1977.
      (*See* B 5.1)

187   Brock, J.
      *A Program for the Preservation of Library Materials in
      the General Library.*
      Berkeley: University of California, 1975.
      (*See* A 2.4)

188   Brookes, B. C.
      "Growth, utility and obsolescence of scientific peri-
      odical literature."
      Journal of Documentation   26 (December 1970):
      283-94.

189   Brouwer, H.
      "Nagmaals: afschrijving van openbaar bibliotheekbezit"
      ("Again: depreciation on public library stock").
      Open 7 (June 1975): 297-301.

190   Brown, M., D. Etherington, and L. McWilliams.
      *Design and Construction of Boxes for the Protection
      of Rare Books.*
      Washington, D. C.: Library of Congress, forthcoming.
      (*See* D 1.1)

191   Brown, Q., and B. Fairley.
      "Repair and maintenance of media equipment and soft-
      ware: a panel presentation."
      In Canadian Association of College and University
      Libraries, *Non-Print Media Problems; Proceedings of a
      Pre-Conference Workshop* (Ottawa: Canadian Library
      Association, 1975), pp. 33-38.   (Canadian Library
      Association Occasional Paper, no. 83.)

      Brown, T. J.
      See 1004, Powell, R.

192   Browning, B. L.
      Analysis of Paper.
      New York: Marcel Dekker, 1969.

193   Browning, B. L.
      "The nature of paper."
      Library Quarterly 40 (January 1970): 18-38.

194   Browning, B. L., and W. A. Wink.
      "Studies on the permanence and durability of paper;
      I: The prediction of paper permanence."
      Tappi 51 (1968): 163-66.

195 Brubaker, R. L.
"Conservation in the midwest: a preliminary report."
Newsletter of the Midwest Archives Conference 5
(July 1977): 35-42.

196 Bruce, J.
"The conservation of archives in Australia."
Archives and Manuscripts 7 (February 1978): 63-71.

197 Bruce, J.
"Restoration and preservation of documents; part 1."
Archives and Manuscripts 5 (May 1974): 179-82.

198 Bruce, J.
"Restoration and preservation of documents; part 2."
Archives and Manuscripts 6 (August 1974): 215-20.

Bruce, J.
See 772, McGregor, L.

199 Brüderlin, P.
Grosse dokumentationsprobleme in der Schweiz;
dokumentare sicherstellung von kulturgütern" ("Large
documentation problems in Switzerland; documentary
safeguarding of cultural objects").
Nachrichten Vereinigung Schweizerischer Bibliothekare
48, 1 (1972): 1-5.

200 Bubbers, J. J.
"What you can do to minimize record wear."
High Fidelity Magazine 22, 9 (1972): 54-55.

201 Buck, R. D.
"Formal procedures: their effect on performance stan-
dards in conservation."
In Timmons, S., ed., *Preservation and Conservation:
Principles and Practices* (Washington D. C.: National
Trust for Historic Preservation in the U. S., Preservation
Press, 1976), pp. 403-19.

202 Buck, R. D.
      "On Conservation; what is a regional conservation center and why?"
      Museum News 52, 8 (1974): 10.
      (*See* A 4.8)

203 Buck, R. D., and others.
      "An investigation into the use of pH indicators on paper."
      Intermuseum Conservation Association Newsletter 7, 1 (1969).

204 Büge, S. R.
      Der Pappband: Ein Brevier für Buchbinder und Bücherfreunde ("The boards: a breviary for bookbinders and bibliophiles").
      Hamburg: H. Christians, 1973.

205 Buick, M.
      "One method of sewing single sheets for binding."
      The Paper Conservator 2 (1977): 4-5.

206 Bullen, R.
      "Books and ecology."
      Unabashed Librarian 3 (Spring 1972): 7-9.

207 Burdett, E.
      "Repairs to books."
      In *The Craft of Bookbinding; A Practical Handbook* (London: David and Charles, 1975), pp. 329-47.
      (*See* D 1.5)

208 Bureau, W. H.
      "Paper formation."
      Graphic Arts Monthly 43, 7 (1971): 60-63.

209 Bureau, W. H.
      "Paper situation: now and ahead."
      Graphic Arts Monthly 47, 2 (1975): 66-69.

210   Bureau, W. H.
        "Paper sizing."
        Graphic Arts Monthly 43, 8 (1971): 86, 88, 90.

211   Bureau, W. H.
        "pH—its meaning and significance."
        Graphic Arts Monthly 44, 6 (1972): 82, 84-85.

212   Bureau, W. H.
        "Recycled and reclaimed—defined."
        Graphic Arts Monthly 44, 11 (1972): 84, 86.

213   Bureau, W. H.
        "Static: unwelcomed guest in paper."
        Graphic Arts Monthly 38, 3 (1966): 108, 110.

214   Bureau, W. H.
        "Waste paper—facts vs. misconceptions."
        Graphic Arts Monthly 44, 7 (1972): 54, 56.

215   Bureau, W. H.
        "Waste paper—facts vs. misconceptions: part 2."
        Graphic Arts Monthly 44, 8 (1972): 58-60.

      Burlinson, C.
        See 343, DeWitt, D. L.

216   Burnham, J. M.
        "Processing and storage of photographic plates for
        permanent records."
        American Astronomical Society Photo Bulletin 1
        (1973): 12-14.

217   Burns, R.
        "Space age drying method salvages library books."
        Fire Engineering 126, 12 (December 1973): 52.

218   Burns, S., and N. J. Root.
        "Restoring and cataloging a rare motion picture collec-
        tion."
        Curator 18, 1 (March 1975): 77-81.

219 Burtseva, T.
"Beregite knigi; konsul'tatsiia" ("Preserve books; recommended practices").
Bibliotekar' no. 11 (1972): 51-54.

220 Butterfield, M. A.
"Care and preservation of the new media: equipment needs."
In University of Denver, *Pioneer Presentation of a National Symposium on the Impact of Automation on Documentation* (Denver: University of Denver, 1968), pp. 60-64.

221 Byrd, C. K.
"Quarters for special collections in university libraries."
Library Trends 18 (1969): 223-34.

222 Byrne, J., and J. Weiner.
Permanence.
Appleton, Wisconsin: Institute of Paper Chemistry, 1964.
(Bibliographic series, no. 213)

C

223 Cains, A.
"New attitudes to conservation."
In Smith, P., *New Directions in Bookbinding* (New York: Van Nostrand Reinhold, 1974), pp. 164-72.
(*See* D 1.6)

224 Cains, A.
"Techniques of preservation based on early binding methods and materials."
The Paper Conservator 1 (1976): 2-8.
(*See* D 3.2)

Cairns, T.
See 603, Johnson, B. B.

225   Calhoun, J. M.
"The preservation of motion picture film."
American Archivist 30 (July 1967): 517-25.
(Technical notes)

226   Califano, E.
*Récupération et Restauration du Patrimoine des
Archives Italiennes Détériorées par les Inondations
du 4 Novembre 1966* ("Recovery and restoration of
the patrimony of Italian archives damaged in the floods
of November 4, 1966").
Rome: Centro di Fotoriproduzione Legatoria e
Restauro, 1968.

227   California Heritage Preservation Commission.
*The Preservation, Organization and Display of
California's Historic Documents: Second Report to the
California State Legislature, February 14, 1967.*
Sacramento: The Commission, 1967.

228   California Library Authority for Systems and Services.
Toward a California Document Conservation Program.
San Jose, California: California Library Authority for
Systems and Services. 1979.

229   Cameron, D.
"Environmental control: a theoretical solution."
Museum News 46,9 (1968): 17-21.
(*See* B 2.9)

Canadian Association of College and University Libraries.
See 191, Brown, Q.

230   Canadian Historical Association. Archives Section. Com-
mittee on the Conservation of Writings.
"Report: 2 June, 1970."
Canadian Archivist 2, 2 (1971): 39-48.

231 Cande, L. N.
"Study of book damage and restoration in the libraries of Florence, Italy."
Research paper, Long Island University, 1970.

232 Capps, M. T.
"Preservation and maintenance of maps."
Special Libraries 63 (October 1972): 457-62.

233 Capps, M. T.
"Preservation and maintenance of maps."
Drexel Library Quarterly 9 (October 1973): 61-70.
Revised version.

234 Carbery, M. G.
"Libraries of Florence after the 1966 flood."
Catholic Library World 41 (October 1969): 94-101.

235 "Care of daguerreotypes and ambrotypes: advice from the Photographic Historical Society of N. Y."
Special Libraries Association, Picture Division
Picturescope 19 (Summer 1971): 93-95.

236 Carhart, F. F.
"Publishing on permanent papers: discussion."
Library Quarterly 40 (January 1970): 122-27.

Carlton, A. M.
See 116, Barrow, W. J.

237 Cassidy, L. B.
"Out of the limelight."
American Libraries 4 (September 1973): 458.
(letter)

238 Castagna, E.
"Last rites: the uneasy business of disposing of bookish remains."
AB Bookman's Weekly 40 (October 2-9, 1967) 1191-92.

239   Castro, J.
       Arte de tratar o livro   ("Art of caring for books").
       Pôrto Alegre: Livraria Sulina Editôra, 1969.

240   "Cause and prevention of microfilm blemishes."
       Records Management Journal   7, 3 (Autumn 1969):
       22-24.

241   Cave, R.
       "The care of restoration of rare books."
       In *Rare Book Librarianship*   (London: Clive Bingley,
       1976), pp. 83-93.

242   "Cellulose nitrate film."
       Journal of the Society of Archivists   4 (April 1970):
       67-68.
       (notes and news)

       Cernia, E.
       See 747, Mark, H. F.

243   Chahine, C., and F. Flieder.
       "Comportement des reliures encuir soumises a` dif-
       férents traitements de désinfection"   ("Behavior of
       bookbinding in leather subjected to different treatments
       of disinfection").
       Studies in Conservation 19 (November 1974): 194-206.

244   Chandler, M.
       "Preservation of government publications."
       In Jordan, A. T., ed. , *Research Library Cooperation in
       the Caribbean* (Chicago: American Library Association,
       1973), pp. 131-38.
       (Papers of the 1st and 2nd meeting of the Association of
       Caribbean University and Research Libraries)

245   Chatters, R. M., and C. Jacobs.
       "Recovery of faded photographs by nuclear tech-
       niques."
       Technology and Medicine 5 (January 1970): 26-27, 47.

246   Chernofsky, J. L.
       "Beta radiography techniques."
       AB Bookman's Weekly 54 (September 16, 1974):1130.

247   Chernofsky, J. L.
       "Manuscript mutilation."
       AB Bookman's Weekly 55 (March 3, 1975): 970.

248   Chernofsky, J. L.
       "Pilfering in libraries."
       AB Bookman's Weekly 56 (September 8, 1975): 946.

249   Chernofsky, J. L.
       "Pre-conference roundup: the care of books and book-
       men."
       AB Bookman's Weekly 54 (July 29, 1974): 459-60.

250   Chernofsky, J. L.
       "Theory and practice."
       AB Bookman's Weekly 54 (October 14, 1974): 1546.

251   Chicago Paper Testing Laboratory.
       "Permanent and durable library catalog cards."
       Library Technology Reports, November 1975.
       (Supplies and miscellaneous)

252   Christiansen, P. A.
       "Report of a conference meeting of the working party
       on the physical protection of books and documents,
       Copenhagen, May 21-22, 1971."
       Restaurator 2 (1972): 29-31.

253   "Chronic shortages ahead for book makers."
       Publishers' Weekly 204 (December 3, 1973): 28-32.

254   Chudaev, A.
       "Chtoby sockhranit' knizhnye fondy" ("Preservation of
       bookstocks").
       Biblioteka 4 (April 1971): 59-62.

255 Chukaev, A.
"Vospityvat' berezhnoe otnoshenie k knigam" ("Educating young readers to handle books carefully"). *Bibliotekar'* no. 1 (1974): 54-57.

Ciecuch, R. F. W.
See 1067, Rodgers, H. G.

256 Clapp, A. F.
Curatorial Care of Works of Art on Paper.
Oberlin, Ohio: Ohio Intermuseum Association, 1978. Third ed., rev.

257 Clapp, A. F.
Reading List for Students in Conservation of Historic and Artistic Works on Paper.
Washington, D. C.: American Institute for Conservation of Historic and Artistic Works, 1976.
(*See* E 1.5)

258 Clapp, V. W.
"Declaration of Independence: a case study in preservation."
Special Libraries 62 (December 1971): 503-508.

259 Clapp, V. W.
Story of Permanent/Durable Book Paper, 1115-1970.
Copenhagen: Restaurator Press, 1972.
(Restaurator Supplement, no. 3)
Also in *Scholarly Publishing* 2 (January 1971): 107-24; (April 1971): 229-45; (July 1971): 353-67.
(*See* E 4.4)

260 Clapperton, R. H.
The Paper-Making Machine: Its Invention, Evolution and Development.
Oxford and New York: Pergamon, 1967.

Clark, R. L.
See 992, Poole, F. G.

261   Clark, W.
      "Techniques for conserving those old photographs."
      New York Times, June 13, 1976, pp. D37-40.

262   Clarke, A.
      "Florence and Venice preserved."
      Apollo 89 (February 1969): 142-43.

263   Clarke, J. A.
      "Popular culture in libraries."
      College and Research Libraries   34 (1973): 215-18.

264   Clarkson, C.
      "Limp vellum binding and its potential use for the
      rebinding of early printed books: a break with 19th
      and 20th century rebinding attitudes and practices."
      Unpublished paper, Washington, D. C., Library of
      Congress, 1972.

265   Clarkson, C.
      "Protective boxes for Near Eastern bookcovers from the
      Minassian collection."
      *Bulletin of the American Institute for Conservation of
      Historic and Artistic Works*   15, 2 (1975): 10-16.

266   Clayton, N. W., and G. H. Fudge.
      "Chemical dehumidification protects microfilm records
      stored in mountain vaults."
      Heating, Piping, and Air Conditioning   38, 10 (1966):
      127-29.

267   "Close-up: what's happening in the bindery?"
      Inland Printer/American Lithographer   172 (April
      1974): 64-67.

268   "Club-soda time capsule."
      Unabashed Librarian 13 (Fall 1974): 30.
      Reprinted from *Time*, September 9, 1974.

269   Cochetti, M.
      "Di alcuni restauri settezenteschi di legature" ("Con-
      cerning several 18th century restorations of bindings").
      Bollettino dell'Istituto di Patologia del Libro 30 (Jan-
      uary-June 1971): 113-18.

270   Cockerell, D.
      Bookbinding and the Care of Books; A Text-Book for Bookbinders and Librarians.
      London: Sir Isaac Pitman and Sons, 1971.
      5th ed. rev.
      (*See* D 3.6)

271   Cockerell, S. M.
      The Repairing of Books.
      London: Sheppard Press, 1958.

272   Cohen, W. M.
      "From the editor's desk: Halon 1301, library fires, and post-alarm procedures."
      Library Security Newsletter 1 (May 1975): 5-7.

273   Cole, J. E.
      "Solvents and their use."
      Records Management Journal 9, 2 (Summer 1971): 21-22.

      College Art Association.
      See 944, Organ, R. M.

274   Collier, V., and J. Hinkle.
      "Emergency—damaged books!"
      Oklahoma Librarian 24 (January 1974): 14-16.

275   Collings, T. J., and F. J. Young.
      "Improvements in some tests and techniques in photograph conservation."
      Studies in Conservation 21 (May 1976): 79-84.

276   Collis, I. P.
      "The use of thymol for document fumigation."
      Journal of the Society of Archivists 4 (April 1970): 53-54.

277   Collison, R. L.
      Commercial and Industrial Records Storage.
      New York: J. deGraff, 1969.

278 Colton, A. S.
"Marbling: an ancient art."
Graphic Arts Monthly 46, 9 (1974): 124-26.

279 Comparato, F. E.
Books for the Millions: A History of the Men Whose Methods and Machines Packaged the Printed Word. Harrisburg, Pennsylvania: The Stackpole Company, 1971.

280 "Conservation at Worcester not up to snuff."
Library Journal 100 (September 15, 1975): 1592-93.

281 "Conservation of research library materials; course arranged by the University of Illinois."
Studies in Conservation 16 (February 1971): 33-34.

282 "Conservation problems: multi-media exhibition called 'Books in Peril.' "
AB Bookman's Weekly 51 (April 9, 1973): 1292.

283 "Conservation resources in South and South-East Asia."
Museum (Unesco) 27, 4 (1975): 205-210.

284 "Conservation topics: dusting and dry cleaning."
Library Security Newsletter 1 (May 1975): 12.

285 "Contributo dell'Istituto di Patologia del Libro al salvataggio del materiale alluvionato della Toscana" ("Contributions of the Institute of Book Pathology in the salvage of materials flooded in Tuscany").
Bolletino dell'Istituto di Patologia del Libro 26 (July-December 1967): 258-61.

286 "Convegno dei Soprintendenti bibliografici sul restauro e la valorizzazione del patrimonio librario nazionale" ("Meeting of Bibliographical Superintendents on the restoration and effective use of the national book heritage").
Associazione Italiana Biblioteche Bollettino d' Informazioni 10 (July-September 1970): 84-86.

287   Cook, M.
      "Conservation of archives."
      In *Archives Administration: A Manual for Intermediate
      and Smaller Organizations and for Local Government*
      (Folkestone, Kent, England: Dawson, 1977), pp. 135-
      43.

288   Cook, W. A.
      Electrostatics in Reprography.
      London and New York: Focal Press, 1970.

      Cooper, D.
      See 1098, Segal, J.

289   Cooper, D. W.
      "Library security: an administrative overview."
      North Carolina Libraries   32 (Winter 1974): 9-17.

290   Corbett, D. J.
      *Motion Picture and Television Film: Image Control and
      Processing Techniques.*
      London and New York: Focal Press, 1968.
      (BBC engineering training manual)

291   Coremans, P.
      "The training of restorers."
      In International Council of Museums, Committee for
      Museum Laboratories, *Problems of Conservation in
      Museums*   (Paris: Editions Eyrolles, 1969), pp. 7-32.

292   Cornell University Libraries.
      CUL Emergency Manual.
      Ithaca, N.Y.: Cornell University Libraries, 1977.
      (*See* B 3.1)

293   "Corso internazionale sulla conservatione dei materiali di
      biblioteca ed archivio" ("International course on
      conservation of library and archival materials").
      Bollettino dell'Istituto di Patologia del Libro   27 (July-
      December 1968): 251-53.
      Also published in *Accademie e Biblioteche d'Italia*
      36 (November 1968): 376-78.

294   Corujeira, L. A.
        Conserve e Resaure Seus Documentos.
        Salvador, Brasil: Editôra Itapuã, 1971.

295   Corujeira, L. A.
        "Métodos de prevençao e eliminaçao de fungos em
        materiais bibliográficos" ("Methods for the prevention
        and elimination of fungi in library materials").
        Revista de Biblioteconomia de Brasilia   1 (January
        1973): 59-65.

296   "Council on Library Resources grant goes to NEILC for
        document conservation."
        Library Journal 98 (March 15, 1973): 821.

297   Crawford, H.
        "Technical processing: preservation of library materi-
        als."
        In Annan, G. L., and J. W. Felter, eds., *Handbook of
        Medical Library Practice*   (Chicago: Medical Library
        Association, 1970), pp. 135-52.

298   Crespo, C.
        *Technical Improvements in the Preservation and Repro-
        duction of Archival Documents.*
        Washington, D. C.: 8th International Congress on
        Archives, 1976.

299   Crocetti, L.
        "Un'esperienza di cooperazione: Centro di restauro
        della Biblioteca nazionale centrale di Firenze" ("An
        experiment in cooperation: Center for restoration at the
        National central library at Florence").
        Bollettino dell'Istituto di Patologia del Libro   29 (Jan-
        uary-December 1970): 27-49.

        Crocker, H.
        See 1088, Santen, V.

300   Cronvall, B.
        ABC i bokvard   ("ABC's in book care").
        3d ed.
        Lund, Sweden: Bibliotekstjanst, 1973.

301   Crook, D. M., and W. E. Bennett.
      *The Effect of Humidity and Temperature on the Phys-
      ical Properties of Paper.*
      Kenley, Surrey, England: The British Paper and Board
      Industry Research Association, 1962.

302   Crowley, A. S.
      "Repair and conservation of palm-leaf manuscripts."
      Restaurator 1 (1969): 105-114.

303   Croxton, F. E.
      "Preserve or not to preserve?"
      Special Libraries 63 (October 1972): 6A-7A.
      (letter)

304   Culp, R. W.
      "Thefts, mutilations, and library exhibits."
      Special Libraries 67 (December 1976): 582-84.
      (*See* B 4.3)

305   Cunha, G. M.
      "Conservation and preservation of archives."
      Paper presented at the SAA/NEH Conference on
      Priorities for Funding, Chicago, January 1977.
      Summarized with discussion in *American Archivist* 40
      (July 1977): 321-24.
      (*See* E 5.3)

306   Cunha, G. M.
      "Conserving local archival materials on a limited
      budget."
      History News   30, 11 (November 1975): 253-264.
      (AASLH technical leaflet 86)

307   Cunha, G. M.
      "An evaluation of recent developments for the mass
      drying of books."
      In Williams, J. C., ed., *Preservation of Paper and Textiles
      of Historical and Artistic Value* (Washington, D. C.:
      American Chemical Society, 1977), pp. 95-104.
      (Advances in Chemistry Series, no. 164)
      (*See* B 3.2)

308   Cunha, G. M.
       "A mobile vacuum fumigator for New England."
       *Bulletin of the American Institute for Conservation of
       Historic and Artistic Works*   14, 2 (1974): 65-68.

309   Cunha, G. M.
       "New England Document Conservation Center program
       report."
       Vermont Libraries 3 (November 1974): 13-15.

310   Cunha, G. M.
       "Preservation and conservation of legal materials."
       Law Library Journal   69 (August 1976): 300-302.

311   Cunha, G. M.
       "Preservation of library materials."
       In American Library Association, *ALA Yearbook*
       (Chicago: ALA, 1976), pp. 265-66.

312   Cunha, G. M.
       "A regional restoration center for New England."
       *Bulletin of the American Institute for Conservation
       of Historic and Artistic Works*   13, 2 (1973): 6-16.

313   Cunha, G. M.
       "Vapor phase deacidification."
       American Archivist   30 (October 1967): 614-15; 31
       (January 1968): 84-86.

314   Cunha, G. M., and D. G. Cunha.
       *Conservation of Library Materials; A Manual and
       Bibliography on the Care, Repair and Restoration of
       Library Materials.*
       Metuchen, New Jersey: Scarecrow Press, 1972.
       2d ed.
       (*See* E 1.7)

315   Cunha, G. M., F. G. Poole, and C. C. Walton.
       "The conservation and preservation of historical
       records."
       American Archivist 40 (July 1977): 321-24.
       (Summaries of papers presented at the SAA/NEH
       Conference on Priorities for Funding, January 1977,
       Chicago)

316   Cunha, G. M., and N. P. Tucker, eds.
       Library and Archives Conservation: The Boston Athenaeum's 1971 Seminar on the Application of Chemical and Physical Methods to the Conservation of Library and Archival Materials: May 17-21, 1971.
       Boston: The Library of the Boston Athenaeum, 1972.
       (*See also* articles from this work, cited separately, by J. E. Kusterer, F. G. Poole, R. H. Potter, and C. R. Wrotenberry.)

       Cunha, G. M.
       See 649, Kowalik, R.; 812, Morrison, R. C.

317   Cunningham, J. K. H.
       "The protection of records and documents against fire."
       Journal of the Society of Archivists 3 (October 1968): 411-17.

318   Currall, H. F. J., ed.
       Gramophone Record Libraries: Their Organization and practice.
       London: Crosby Lockwood, 1970.
       2d ed.

319   Cutter, C.
       "The restoration of paper documents and manuscripts."
       College and Research Libraries 28, 6 (November 1967): 387-97.

                                    D

320   D'Acunti, E.
       Cristoforo Marino, un geniale napoletano tra documenti antichi.
       Napoli: F. Fiorentino, 1973.

321 Dadić, V.
      "Izbor termoplasticna mase za restauriranje bibliotecne
      grade" ("Choice of thermoplastic films for the preserva-
      tion of library material").
      Vjesnik Bibliotekara Hrvatske 14, 1-2 (1968): 48-53.

322 Dadić, V., and T. Ribkin.
      "Techniques of delaminating polyethylene laminates."
      Restaurator 1 (1970): 141-48.

323 D'Alleyrand, M. R.
      "Microfilming continuous tone materials."
      American Archivist 39 (October 1976): 515-19.
      (Technical notes)
      (*See* C 2.3)

      Daniel, E. D.
      See 383, Eldridge, P. F.

324 Daniels, V.
      "Elimination of bleaching agents from paper."
      The Paper Conservator 1 (1976): 9-11.

325 Darling, P. W.
      "Books in peril; a local preservation program: where
      to start."
      Library Journal 101 (November 15, 1976): 2343-47.
      (*See* A 1.1)

326 Darling, P. W.
      "Developing a preservation microfilming program."
      Library Journal 99 (November 1, 1974): 2803-09.
      Abridged version reprinted in Diaz, A. J., ed., *Micro-
      forms in Libraries* (Weston, Connecticut: Microform
      Review, 1975).
      (*See* C 3.8)

327 Darling, P. W.
      "Microforms in libraries: preservation and storage."
      Microform Review 5 (April 1976): 93-100.
      (*See* C 1.2)

328   Darling, P. W.
        "Preservation: a national plan at last?"
        Library Journal   102 (February 15, 1977): 447-49.
        (*See* A 4.3)

      Darling, P. W.
        See 964, Patton, F.

329   Datta, D. G.
        "Care and preservation of rare library materials."
        *Indian Associations of Special Libraries and Information
        Centres Bulletin*   14, 3 (September 1969): 97-101.

330   Daugherty, P. M.
        "Composition of ball pen inks."
        In English, D. N., and J. M. English, eds., *Proceedings
        of the First Georgetown Conference on Surface
        Analysis, Washington, D. C., 1969*
        (Washington, D. C.: Georgetown University Law Center,
        1970), pp. 16-24.

331   Daum, J.
        Insekten als Schädlinge in Bibliotheken.
        Wiesbaden: Harrassowitz, 1977.

332   Davenport, C. J. H.
        "Paper."
        In *The Book: Its History and Development* (Detroit:
        Tower Books, 1971), pp. 62-84.
        (Reprint of the 1908 edition)

333   Davies, J.
        "Conservation of records with particular reference to
        Malaysia."
        Southeast Asian Archives 4 (July 1971): 28-40.
        Abstract in *American Archivist*   35 (July-October
        1972): 427.

334   Davies, J.
        *A Study of Basic Standards and Methods in Preservation
        and Restoration Workshops Applicable to Developing
        Countries.*
        Brussels: International Council on Archives with the
        cooperation of Unesco, 1973.

335   Davis, L. E.
      Preservation of Machine-Readable Records.
      Washington, D. C.: National Archives and Records
      Service, 1969.

336   Davison, P. S., P. Giles, and D. A. R. Matthews.
      "Aging of magnetic tape: a critical bibliography and
      comparison of literature sources."
      Computer Journal 2 (1968): 241-46.

337   Dearstyne, B. W.
      "Microfilming historical records: an introduction."
      History News 32, 6 (June 1977): 155-62.
      (AASLH technical leaflet 96)

338   Dela Rosa, A. V.
      "Hand Binder says."
      Wisconsin Library Bulletin 72 (November-December
      1976): 275.

339   Denel, F.
      "Une experience de microfilmage de substitution"
      ("An experiment in substitution microfilming").
      Gazette des Archives 83 (1973): 223-227.

340   Department of Agriculture.
      Silverfish and Firebrats: How to Control Them.
      Washington, D. C.: Government Printing Office, 1966.
      (USDA leaflet, no. 412)

341   Deschin, J.
      "M.I.T. starts archival photographic collection."
      New York Times, April 7, 1968, sect. 11, p. 31.

342   DeSomogyi, A.
      "Access versus preservation."
      Canadian Library Journal 31 (October 1974): 414-15.

343   DeWitt, D. L., and C. Burlinson.
      "Leather bookbindings: preservation techniques."
      History News 32, 8 (August 1977): 205-18.
      (AASLH technical leaflet 98)

344   Di Franco Lilli, M. C.
      "Conservazione e restauro; problemi della 'Nazionale'
      di Rio de Janeiro" ("Conservation and restoration;
      problems of the National Library of Rio de Janeiro").
      Accademie e Biblioteche d'Italia 42 (November 1974):
      483-89.

      di Trapani, R.
      See 1232, Triolo, L.

345   Diaz, A. J.
      "Microform information sources: publications and
      hardware."
      Microform Review 4 (October 1975): 250-61.
      (*See* C 3.5)

346   Diaz, A. J., ed.
      Microforms in Labraries: A Reader.
      Weston, Connecticut: Microform Review, 1975.
      (*See also* article from this work, cited separately, by
      P. W. Darling.)
      (*See* C 3.3)

      Diaz, A. J.
      See 1109, Shepard, G. F.

347   Dietze, J.
      "Konservierung und restaurierung von büchern in den
      sozialistischen   ländern: ein   symposiums—bericht"
      ("Conservation and restoration of books in the socialist
      countries: a report on a symposium").
      Zentralblatt für Bibliothekswesen 86 (March 1972):
      164-66.

348   "Disposal of microfilmed records, microfilm storage and
      filming standards, criteria for using microfilm copies,
      and microfilm services available from GSA."
      Federal Register 37 (February 10, 1972): 2962-64.
      (Amendment to Part 101-11 of Title 41 of the *Code
      of Federal Regulations*)

349 Dobi, S.
    "Restoring Robert Flaherty's 'Nanook of the North'."
    Film Library Quarterly 10, 1-2 (1977): 6-18.

350 Dolloff, F. W., and R. Perkinson.
    How to Care for Works of Art on Paper.
    Boston: Museum of Fine Arts, 1971.

351 Doms, K., ed.
    "Preservation of library materials."
    Pennsylvania Library Association Bulletin 28 (November 1973): 219-51.
    (*See also* articles from this issue, cited separately, by R. L. Feller, A. H. Rineer, and W. Spawn.)
    (*See* E 5.6)

352 "Dopo l'alluvione" ("After the flood").
    Accademie e Biblioteche d'Italia 35 (January 1967): 4-16.

353 Douglas, R. A.
    "A commonsense approach to environmental control."
    Curator 15 (1972): 139-44.

354 Dowling, J. H., and C. B. Ford.
    "Halon 1301 total flooding system for Winterthur Museum."
    Fire Journal 63, 6 (November 1969): 10-14.
    (*See* subsequent article by C. B. Ford.)

    Dranov, P.
    See 1039, Reed, J. R.

355 Drayman, T.
    "Conservation of a Petrarch manuscript."
    Walters Art Gallery Journal 31-32 (1968-1969): 119-23.

356 Draznoiwsky, R.
    "Map storage and preservation."
    In *Map Librarianship: Readings* (Metuchen, New Jersey: Scarecrow, 1975), pp. 359-410.

(*See also* articles from this work, cited separately, by P. G. Alonso, C. I. Bahn, R. I. Boak, M. Galneder, and R. D. Smith.)

Duchein, M.
See 434, Flieder, F.

357   Duckett, K. W.
"Physical care and conservation."
In *Modern Manuscripts: A Practical Manual for their Management, Care, and Use.* (Nashville: American Association for State and Local History, 1975), pp. 86-112.
(*See* E 3.2)

Dudley, D. H.
See 967, Pearson, V.; 1172, Stolow, N.

358   Dupuis, R. N., J. E. Kusterer, and R. C. Sproull.
"Evaluation of Langwell's vapor phase deacidification process."
Restaurator 1 (1970): 149-64.
Also published in *Library of Congress Information Bulletin* 29 (1970): A41-A43.

359   Durst, R. A.
Standard Reference Materials: Standardization of pH Measurements.
Washington, D. C.: Government Printing Office, 1975.

E

360   "Earthquake!"
Records Management Quarterly 5 (July 1971): 24-27.

361   "Earthquake in L. A.: damage and a lesson."
Library Journal 96 (March 15, 1971): 906-907.

362 East Street Gallery.
Procedures for Processing and Storing Black and White Photographs for Maxium Possible Permanence.
Grinnell, Iowa: East Street Gallery, 1970.
(*See* D 6.8)

East Street Gallery.
See 1326, Wilhelm, H.

363 "East Street Gallery of Grinnell, Iowa: its successful professional approach to archival permanence of black and white photographic prints."
Special Libraries Association, Picture Division *Picturescope* 19 (Summer 1971): 100-102.

364 Eastman Kodak Company.
Black/White Processing for Permanence.
Rochester, New York: Eastman Kodak Company 1976.
(Kodak publication J-19)

365 Eastman Kodak Company.
Control Procedures in Microfilm Processing.
Rochester, New York: Eastman Kodak Company, 1974.
(Kodak publication D-17)

366 Eastman Kodak Company.
Copying.
Rochester, New York: Eastman Kodak Company, 1974.
(Kodak publication M-1)

367 Eastman Kodak Company.
Handling and Storage of Kodak and Eastman Motion Picture Films.
Rochester, New York: Eastman Kodak Company, 1975.
(Kodak publication D-23)

368 Eastman Kodak Company.
Kodak Darkroom Dataguide.
Rochester, New York: Eastman Kodak Company, 1976.
(Kodak publication R-20)

369   Eastman Kodak Company.
      Kodak Dye Transfer Process.
      Rochester, New York: Eastman Kodak Company, 1976.
      (Kodak publication E-80)

370   Eastman Kodak Company.
      Preservation of Photographs.
      Rochester, New York: Eastman Kodak Company.
      (Kodak publication F-30, forthcoming in 1978)

371   Eastman Kodak Company.
      *Prevention and Removal of Fungus on Prints and
      Films.*
      Rochester, New York: Eastman Kodak Company, 1974.
      (Kodak publication AE-22)

372   Eastman Kodak Company.
      Processing Chemicals and Formulas.
      Rochester, New York: Eastman Kodak Company, 1977.
      (Kodak publication J-1)

373   Eastman Kodak Company.
      Storage and Preservation of Microfilms.
      Rochester, New York: Eastman Kodak Company, 1976.
      (Kodak publication D-31)
      (*See* C 1.6)

374   Eastman Kodak Company.
      Videofilm Notes.
      Rochester, New York: Eastman Kodak Company, 1976.
      (Kodak publication H-40-9)

375   Easton, W. W.
      "Repair and preservation of map materials."
      Special Libraries 61 (April 1970): 199-200.

376   Eaton, G. T.
      "Preservation, deterioration, restoration of photo-
      graphic images."
      Library Quarterly 40 (January 1970): 85-98.

377 Echazú Lezica, M. de.
"Preservación y restauración de fondos documentales"
("Preservation and restoration of basic documents").
Revista del Archivo General de la Nacion 3, 3 (1973):
33-48.

378 Edelglass, E. T., S. C. Strom, and S. J. Turner, comps.
"Writings on archives, historical manuscripts, and
current records: 1975."
American Archivist 40 (April 1977): 207-33.
(*See* E 1.1)

379 Edwards, C. J., F. L. Hudson, and J. A. Hockey.
"Sorption of sulphur dioxide by paper."
Journal of Applied Chemistry 18 (1968): 146-48.

380 Edwards, D.
"Old maps made new: Harry Margary's methods."
Penrose Annual 69 (1976): 188-201.

381 Edwards, M. J.
"The conversion confusion: some comments."
Journal of Micrographics 9 (July-August 1976):
287-89.

382 Ehrenberg, R.
"Reproducing maps in libraries and archives: the custo-
dian's point of view."
Special Libraries 64 (January 1973): 18, 20-24.

383 Eldridge, P. F., and E. D. Daniel.
"Causes of failure in magnetic tape."
In Pear, C. B., ed., *Magnetic Recording in Science and
Industry* (New York: Reinhold, 1967).
Also published as Memorex Monograph no. 3 (Santa
Clara, California: Memorex Corporation, n. d.)

384 Eley, W.
"Framing paper artifacts."
Paper Conservation News (H. Wayne Eley Assoc., Inc.)
1, 2 (July 1973): 1-4.

385   Eley, W.
      "New conservation studio for Yale University Library."
      Paper Conservation News (H. Wayne Eley Assoc., Inc.)
      1, 6 (March 1974): 1-4.

386   Eley, W.
      "Vapor phase process of mass deacidification of paper
      and books developed."
      Paper Conservation News (H. Wayne Eley Assoc., Inc.)
      1, 4 (November 1973): 1-4.

      Eley, W.
      See 68, Baer, N. S.; 451, Friedman, H. B.

387   Elliott, R. G. H.
      "Leather as a bookbinding material."
      Designers Bookbinders Review   2 (Autumn 1973):
      2-8, 3 (Spring 1974): 11-16; 4 (Autumn 1974): 11-15.
      (*See* D 2.3)

388   Elliott, R. G. H.
      "Long-term durability test for bookbinding leathers;
      a review."
      Journal of the Society of Leather Trades Chemists 53
      (1969): 309-17.

389   Ellsworth, R. E.
      Academic Library Buildings.
      Boulder, Colorado: The Colorado Associated University
      Press, 1973.

390   Ellsworth, R. E.
      *The Economics of Book Storage in College and Univer-
      sity Libraries.*
      Metuchen, New Jersey: Association of Research
      Libraries and Scarecrow Press, 1969.

391   Ellsworth, R. E.
      *Planning the College and University Library Building:
      A Book for Campus Planners and Architects.*
      Boulder, Colorado: Pruett, 1968.
      2d ed.

Elphick, J. J.
See 1284, Walters, A. H.

English, D. N., and J. M. English.
See 88, Banks, P. N.; 330, Daugherty, P. M.

392   Enyeart, J. L.
"Reviving a dagerureotype."
Photographic Journal 110 (September 1970): 338-44.

393   "Et udvalg har undersøgt: Indbindings Centralens service
overfor bibliotekerne; her bringes udvalgets rapport"
("Committee has studied center for binding services
to libraries; here is the report").
Bogens Verden 56, 4-5 (1974): 98-101.

Etherington, D.
See 190, Brown, M.

394   Ettlinger, J. R.
"Binding: bound to last?"
Canadian Library Journal 31 (December 1974): 550-56.
Also published in *Library Scene* 4 (June 1975): 4-6.

395   *Etudes concernant la restaruation d'archives, de livres et
de manuscrits/Studies over restauratie van archief,
boeken en handschriften* ("Studies concerning the
restoration of archives, books and manuscripts").
Brussels: Bibliotheque Royale de Belgique, 1974.
(Archives et bibliothèques de Belgique, numero special
12)

396   "Euthanasia for old books."
Library News Bulletin 39 (July 1972): 274-75.

397   Evanoff, P. C.
"It's the humidity!"
Business Graphics 3, 12 (December 1969): 9-10.

398   Evanoff, P. C., and F. W. Goetz.
"A study of factors affecting book opening."
Book Production Industry 52, 2 (1976): 39-51.

399   Evans, F. B., comp.
      "Preservation: buildings and storage facilities" and
      "Preservation: repair and restoration."
      In *Modern Archives and Manuscripts: A Select Biblio-
      graphy* (Washington, D. C.: Society of American
      Archivists, 1975).
      (*See* E 1.6)

      Evans, N.
      See 141, Berger, R.

400   Everson, W. K.
      "Film treasure trove; the film preservation program at
      20th Century Fox."
      Films in Review 25 (December 1974): 595-610.

401   "Evolving pamphlet bindery: only the strong will survive."
      Inland Printer/American Lithographer 173 (September
      1974): 75-76.

402   "Exhibit of treasures from the Rosenwald collection opened
      at Library, February 10."
      Library of Congress Information Bulletin 32 (1973):
      51-54.

F

403   Fahnestock, C.
      "Survey of preservation practices in historical society
      libraries of New York and New England."
      Research paper, Long Island University, 1970.

      Fairley, B.
      See 191, Brown, Q.

404   Falconer, J. O.
      "Do-it-yourself music binding."
      Wilson Library Bulletin 48 (December 1973): 332-35.

Falconer, W. E.
See 640, King, A.

405 Farkas, A.
"Random thoughts on binding, binderies, librarians, library schools and other related matters."
Library Scene 5 (June 1976): 14-17.
(*See* D 4.2)

Farnsworth, D. S.
See 637, Keyes, K. M.

406 Fauser, A.
Empfehlungen für die Buchrestaurierung.
Kiel: Verein Deutscher Bibliothekare, 1970.

407 Faxon, W. O., and R. E. Fogg.
"Mechanics of adhesive binding."
Penrose Annual 59 (1966): 203-209.

408 Feinberg, L. I.
"Papyrus preservation and discovery at Columbia."
Columbia Library Columns 18 (May 1969): 31-38.

409 Feldman, Mrs. H. A.
"How librarians can help binders give better service."
Library Scene 4 (September 1975): 9-10.
Reprinted from *Library Binder* (May 1959).

410 Feller, R. L.
"Control of deteriorating effects of light on museum objects: heating effects of illumination by incandescent lamps."
Museum News 46, 9 (1968): 39-47.
(*See* B 2.8)

411 Feller, R. L.
"Thermochemically activated oxidation: Mother Nature's book burning."
In Doms, K., ed., "Preservation of library materials,"
Pennsylvania Library Association Bulletin 28 (November 1973), pp. 232-42.

Felter, J. W.
See 297, Crawford, H.

412 Feret, B. L.
"Back to student rip-offs: a point of sale."
Wilson Library Bulletin 47 (September 1972): 46-47.
(*See* B 4.9)

413 Ferry, F. de.
"Le microfilm dans les archives; aspects techniques"
("Microfilm in archives; technical aspects").
Gazette des Archives 67 (1969): 257-91.
Abstract in *American Archivist* 33 (October 1970): 422.

414 Filby, P. W.
"Techniques of exhibitions."
AB Bookman's Yearbook, Part 2 (1968): 8-10.

415 Finzi, J. C., and C. G. LaHood.
"Colloquium on the care and photographic reproduction of manuscripts and rare books, Vatican City, Rome, October 21-24, 1975."
Library of Congress Information Bulletin 34 (December 26, 1975): A137-39.

416 "Fire and flood bulletin: New England libraries hit."
Library Journal 101 (January 15, 1976): 299-300.

417 "Fire rated top problem in security study."
Library Journal 98 (October 15, 1973): 2954.

418 "Fire security problems; prevention and cures."
Library Journal 100 (December 1, 1975): 2203-2204.

419 "First-aid for Florence."
Archives 8 (April 1967): 24-25.

420 Fischer, A.
Das Buchklima.
Kiel: Verein deutscher Bibliothekare, 1969.

421   Fischer, D. J.
      "Conservation research: fumigation and sterilization of
      flood-contaminated library, office, photographic, and
      archival materials."
      In Williams, J. C., ed., *Preservation of Paper and Textiles
      of Historical and Artistic Value* (Washington, D. C.:
      American Chemical Society, 1977), pp. 139-48.
      (Advances in Chemistry Series, no. 164)

422   Fischer, D. J.
      "Conservation Research: use of dielectric and micro-
      wave energy to thaw and dry frozen library materials."
      In Williams, J. C., ed., *Preservation of Paper and Textiles
      of Historical and Artistic Value* (Washington, D. C.:
      American Chemical Society, 1977), pp. 124-38.
      (Advances in Chemistry Series, no. 164)

423   Fischer, D. J.
      "Problems encountered, Hurricane Agnes flood,
      June 23, 1975 at Corning, New York and the Corning
      Museum of Glass."
      In Morrison, R. C., G. M. Cunha, and N. P. Tucker, eds.,
      *Conservation Administration; Seminar on the Theor-
      etical Aspects of the Conservation of Library and
      Archival Materials and the Establishment of Conserva-
      tion Programs, North Andover, Massachusetts, 1973*
      (North Andover, Massachusetts: New England Docu-
      ment Conservation Center and the Library of the
      Boston Athenaeum, 1975), pp. 170-87.

424   Fischer, D. J.
      "Restoration of flood-damaged materials in a special
      library."
      In Morrison, R. C., G. M. Cunha, and N. P. Tucker, eds.,
      *Conservation Administration; Seminar on the Theoret-
      ical Aspects of the Conservation of Library and Archival
      Materials and the Establishment of Conservation
      Programs, North Andover, Massachusetts, 1973* (North
      Andover, Massachusetts: New England Document
      Conservation Center and the Library of the Boston
      Athenaeum, 1975), pp. 137-50.

425   Fischer, D. J.
       "Simulation of flood for preparing reproducible water-
       damaged books and evaluation of traditional and new
       drying methods."
       In Williams, J. C., ed., *Preservation of Paper and Textiles
       of Historical and Artistic Value* (Washington, D. C.:
       American Chemical Society, 1977), pp. 105-23.
       (Advances in Chemistry Series, no. 164)

426   Fischer, K.
       "Exaktni meřeni optických vlastnosti archiválii a jinych
       památek" ("Measuring optical characteristics of records
       and other historical materials").
       Archivni Casopis 3 (1966): 149-53.
       Abstract in *American Archivist* 31 (April 1968): 199.

427   Fitch, J. M.
       "On formulating new parameters for preservation
       policy."
       In Timmons, S., ed., *Preservation and Conservation:
       Principles and Practices* (Washington, D. C.: National
       Trust for Historic Preservation in the U. S., Preservation
       Press, 1976), pp. 311-25.

       Fleck, G.
       See 1089, Sargent, R.

428   Flieder, F.
       "Le centre de recherches sur la protection des docu-
       ments graphiques" ("Center for research on the protec-
       tion of graphic documents").
       Bulletin des Bibliothèques de France 11 (May 1966):
       183-88.

429   Flieder, F.
       *Tunisie: Bibliothèque Nationale et Archives Générales:
       Protection Physique des Manuscrits et des Fonds d'
       Archives, Décember 1973* ("Tunisia: National Library
       and General Archives: Physical protection of manu-
       scripts and the basic collections of archives").
       Paris: Unesco, 1974.

430 Flieder, F.
La Conservation des Documents Graphiques:Recherches Expérimentals ("Conservation of graphic documents: experimental researches").
Paris: Editions Eyrolles, 1969.

431 Flieder, F.
"Le centre de recherches sur la conservation des documents graphiques, Paris" ("Center for research on the conservation of graphic documents").
Studies in Conservation 20 (February 1975): 20-29.

432 Flieder, F.
"Le centre de recherches sur la conservation des documents graphiques" ("Center for research on the conservation of graphic documents").
Caribbean Archives (1974): 37-42.
Reprinted from *Courrier du CNRS* 12 (April 1974).

433 Flieder, F.
"Le centre de recherches sur la conservation des documents graphiques" ("Center for research on the conservation of graphic documents").
Bulletin des Bibliothèques de France 17 (July 1972): 309-20.

434 Flieder, F., and M. Duchein.
"La désinfection des documents d'archives attaqués par les microorganismes et les insectes" ("The disinfection of archival documents attacked by microorganisms and insects").
Gazette des Archives 87 (1974): 225-37.

Flieder, F.
See 243, Chahine, C.

435 Flink, J.
"Utilization of freeze-drying to save water-damaged manuscripts."
Vacuum 22 (July 1972): 273.

436   Flink, J., and H. Hoyer.
       "Conservation of water-damaged written documents by
       freeze-drying."
       Nature 234 (December 1971): 420.
       Summary in *American Archivist* 35 (July-October
       1972): 443-44.

       Flink, J.
       See 1205, Thomas, D.

437   "Floods damage collection."
       AB Bookman's Weekly 56 (September 22-29, 1975):
       1231-32.

438   "Floods ravage Pennsylvania and New York Libraries."
       Library Journal 97 (August 1972): 2511-12.

439   "Florence."
       Book Collector 16 (Spring 1967): 7-43.
       (Special issue)

440   *Florence Rises From the Flood.*
       Chicago: R. R. Donnelley, 1967.

441   Flyate, D. M., ed.
       Preservation of Documents and Papers.
       Jerusalem: Israel Program for Scientific Translations,
       1968.
       (Publication of the USSR Academy of Sciences, Labora-
       tory for the Preservation and Restoration of Docu-
       ments)

       Fogg, R. E.
       See 407, Faxon, W. O.

442   Foramitti, H.
       "Kulturgüterschutz in bibliotheken" ("Protection of
       cultural objects in libraries").
       Biblos 21, 1 (1972): 8-16.

443   Ford, C. B.
      "Winterthur revisited."
      Fire Journal 69, 1 (January 1975): 81-82.

      Ford, C. B.
      See 354, Dowling, J. H.

444   "Formation of a consertium for the microfilming of manuscript and documentary collection in the Australian state archives."
      Library of Congress Information Bulletin 29 (July 9, 1970): 344.

      Fosse, B.
      See 1312, Wendelbo, Ø.

445   Franklin, A. T.
      "Printing paper progress."
      Penrose Annual 67 (1974): 199-204.

446   Frattarolo, C.
      "La situazione delle biblioteche della Toscana e del Veneto ad un anno dall'alluvione" ("Situation of the libraries of Tuscany and Venice a year after the flood").
      Accademie e Biblioteche d'Italia 35 (November 1967): 510-515.

447   "Freeze-dried history."
      Newsweek 79 (January 10, 1972): 39.

448   Freitag, D.
      "Conservation of library materials at Harvard."
      Guild of Book Workers Journal 14 (Fall 1975): 3-5.

449   Friedman, H. B.
      "Preservation of library materials; the state of the art."
      Special Libraries 59 (October 1968): 608-13.

450   Friedman, H. B.
      "Preservation programs in New York state; existent and non-existent."
      Special Libraries 60 (November 1969): 578-89.

451 Friedman, H. B., and W. Eley, eds.
Conservation of Library Materials; A Suggested Reading List.
New York: New York Public Library, 1973.

452 Frost, G.
"Conservation standard rebinding of single books: a review of current practice at the Newberry Library."
AIC Preprints (1977): 56-61.
(Paper presented at the 5th annual meeting of the American Institute for Conservation of Historic and Artistic Works)
(*See* D 3.1)

Fudge, G. H.
See 266, Clayton, N. W.

453 "Fumigator."
Library Technology Reports, September 1972.
(New Products)

Futernick, R.
See 971, Perkinson, R.

G

454 Gaehde, C. M.
"The care and conservation of fine prints."
In Zigrosser, C., and C. M. Gaehde, *A Guide to the Collecting and Care of Original Prints* (New York: Crown Publishers for the Print Council of America, 1965), ch. 7.

Gaehde, C. M.
See 1364, Zigrosser, C.

Gaherty, S.
See 1225, Trelles, O. M.

455 Gallo, F.
"Attivita del laboratorio di biologia dell'Istituto di patologia del libro dal 1961 al 1972" ("Activity of the biology laboratory of the institute of book pathology from 1961 to 1972").
Bollettino dell'Istituto di Patologia del Libro 31 (July-December 1972): 99-113.
biblio.

456 Gallo, F.
"Trattamento con gli alcooli dei materiali librari danneggiati dai microorganism" ("Alcohol treatment of book materials damaged by microorganisms").
Bollettino dell'Istituto di Patologia del Libro 30 (July-December 1971): 123-34.

457 Gallo, F., and P. Gallo.
"Disinfeczione dei libri con ossido di etilene e formaldeide" ("Fumigation of books with ethylene oxide and formaldehyde").
Bollettino dell'Istituto di Patologia del Libro 30 (January-June 1971): 35-69.

458 Gallo, F., and P. Gallo.
"Insetti e microorganismi nemici dei libri" ("Insect and microorganism enemies of books").
Bollettino dell'Istituto di Patologia del Libro 26 (July-December 1967): 143-90.

459 Galneder, M.
"Equipment for map libraries."
In Drazniowsky, R., ed., *Map Librarianship: Readings* (Metuchen, New Jersey: Scarecrow, 1975), pp. 389-94.
Reprinted from *Special Libraries* 61 (July-August 1970): 271-74.

460 Gamer, N.
"℞ for ailing collections; a one-day course at the Medical library convention."
Alabama Librarian 27 (January 1976): 8-9.

461   Gapit, E. B.
        "Techniques of preserving materials."
        ASLP Bulletin 15 (June 1969): 50-57.

462   Gardiner, A. W.
        Typewriting and Office Duplicating Processes.
        New York: Hastings House, 1968.

        Gardner, J. C.
        See 775, McKeon, D. B.

463   Garsed, E. B.
        "Microfilming microfilm: a photochromic process."
        Penrose Annual 64 (1971): 137-43.

464   Garver, T. H.
        "Control of atmospheric pollutants and maintenance of
        stable climatic conditions within museum buildings."
        In Thomson, G., ed., *Contributions to the London
        Conference on Museum Climatology, 18-23 September
        1967* (London: International Institute for Conservation
        of Historic and Artistic Works, 1968).

465   Gear, J. L., R. H. MacClaren, and M. McKiel.
        "Film recovery of some deteriorated black and white
        negatives."
        American Archivist 40 (July 1977): 363-68.
        (Technical notes)
        (*See* D 6.2)

        Gear, J. L.
        See 1341 and 1343, Wilson, W. K.

466   General Services Administration. Accident and Fire Preven-
        tion Division. Advisory Committee on the Protection
        of Archives and Records Centers.
        Protecting Federal Records Centers From Fire.
        Washington, D. C.: Government Printing Office, 1977.
        (*See* B 3.3)

467 Gentile, R. B.
"On the reading of very old magnetic tapes."
Datamation 19 (October 1973): 58-62.

468 Georgia Department of Archives and History. Restoration Section.
Restoring and Preserving Official Documents, Manuscripts, Books, and Maps: Techniques.
Atlanta: Georgia Department of Archives and History, 1972.

469 Gichtel, P.
Der Codex Aureus von St. Emmeram: die Restaurierung des Cod. lat. 14000 der Bayerischen Staatsbibliothek München ("The Codex Aureus of St. Emmeram: the restoration of the Latin Codex 14000 of the Bavarian State Library, Munich").
Munich: Callwey, 1971.

470 Giles, C. H., and R. Haslam.
"The keeping properties of some colour photographs." In Royal Photographic Society of Great Britain, *The Conservation of Colour Photographic Records* (London: Royal Photographic Society of Great Britain, 1974).

Giles, P.
See 336, Davison, P. S.

471 Gilmore, M. P.
"Progress of restoration in Florence."
Renaissance Quarterly 20, 1 (Spring 1967): 96-108.

472 Giuliani, G.
"Termiti all'attacco degli archivi; quindici anni di lotta antitermitica" ("Termites on the attack in archives; fifteen years of antitermite struggle").
Bolletino dell'Istituto di Patologia del Libro 27 (July-December 1968): 181-99.

473 Glaser, M. T.
Framing and Preservation of Works of Art on Paper.
London: Sotheby Parke Bernet, 1972.

474   Goetz, A. H.
       "Books in peril, a history of horrid catastrophes."
       Wilson Library Bulletin   47 (January 1973): 428-39.

       Goetz, F. W.
       See 398, Evanoff, P. C.

475   Gondos, V., ed.
       Reader for Archives and Records Center Buildings.
       Washington: Committee on Archival Buildings and
       Equipment, Society of American Archivists, 1970.

476   "Government Printing Office restoration shops transferred
       to LC supervision."
       Library of Congress Information Bulletin   27 (June 27,
       1968): 342-43.

477   Grady, M. P.
       "Appeal from Florence."
       Catholic Library World   38 (February 1967): 365-68.

478   Grannis, C. B.
       "Reclaimed fibers for quality printing."
       Publishers' Weekly   201 (January 3, 1972): 48-49.

479   Green, K.
       "A group of archives rescued from war-damaged Port
       Moresby."
       Archives and Manuscripts 3 (May 1969): 23-30.

480   Green, S. B.
       "The making of the paper."
       Penrose Annual 69 (1976): 215-18.

481   Greenfield, M. E.
       "Mylar envelopes."
       Guild of Book Workers Journal   11, 3 (1973): 23-27.
       (*See* D 1.7)

482   Greenfeld, H.
       The Waters of November.
       Chicago: Follett, 1969.

Grevel, H.
    See 172, Bouchot, H.

Grim, R. W.
    See 660, Kurth, W. H.

483 Grivainis, I.
     "Appearance of your bookstock."
     Cape Librarian (January 1967): 15.

484 Grove, L. E.
     "John Murray and paper deterioration."
     Libri 16, 3 (1966): 194-204.

485 "Guarding against disaster."
     Law Library Journal 66 (November 1973): 419-28.

486 Guinan, A., and others.
     "Nippur rebaked: the conservation of cuneiform
     tablets."
     Expedition 18, 3 (Spring 1976): 42-47.

487 Guldbeck, P. E.
     *The Care of Historical Collections: a conservation hand-
     book for the nonspecialist.*
     Nashville: American Association for State and Local
     History, 1972.

488 Guldbeck, P. E.
     "Leather: its understanding and care."
     History News 24, 4 (April 1969): 75-86.
     (AASLH technical leaflet 1)

489 Gunner, J.
     "Conservation of library materials at the Hunt Insti-
     tute."
     Guild of Book Workers Journal 14 (Fall 1975): 6-8.

490 Gunner, J.
     "Restoration of books."
     AB Bookman's Weekly 55 (February 3, 1975): 459-60.

491 Gupta, R. C.
"An approach to preservation of photographic materials."
Indian Archives 19 (January-June 1970): 11-12.

492 Gupta, R. C.
"Restoration of documents in Hungary and the GDR."
Conservation of Cultural Property in India 6 (1973): 33-35.

493 Gupta, R. C., and R. Kishore.
"Effect of clenofix and common insecticides on the durability of paper."
Indian Archives 16 (January 1965-December 1966): 29-34.

494 Gupta, R. C., and R. Kishore.
"Effects of alternate heating and cooling on the physical properties of paper."
Indian Archives 19 (July-December 1970): 25-28.

495 Gut, C.
"Restauration des documents d'archives" ("Restoration of archival documents").
In Conférences Internationales de la Table Ronde des Archives, *Actes des onzième et douzième conférences* (Bucharest, 1969), pp. 66-75.

496 Gwinn, N. E.
"The Council of Library Resources; a twenty year report-preservation and microforms."
Library Journal 102 (February 1, 1977): 330-334.

H

497 Haagen-Smit, A. J.
"Air pollution and preservation of art."
In International Institute for Conservation of Historic

and Artistic Works—American Group, *Technical Papers From 1968 Through 1970* (New York: IIC—AG, 1970), pp. 5-13.

498 Haggen-Smit, A. J.
"The chemistry of atmospheric pollution."
In Thomson, G., ed., *Contributions to the London Conference on Museum Climatology, 18-23 September 1967* (London: International Institute for Conservation of Historic and Artistic Works, 1968), pp. 89-94.

499 Haas, W. J.
Preparation of Detailed Specifications for a National System for the Preservation of Library Materials. Washington, D. C.: Association of Research Libraries, 1972.
Reprinted in *Information—Part 2: Reports, Bibliographies* 2, 1-2 (1973): 17-37.
(*See* A 4.9)

500 Haas, W. J.
"Tragedy about to happen: the deterioration of book paper."
Columbia Library Columns 22 (November 1972): 22-27.

501 Hall, D.
"Phonorecord preservation; notes of a pragmatist."
Special Libraries 62 (September 1971): 357-62.
(*See* D 6.7)

Hall, E. T.
See 1214, Thomson, G.

502 Halsey, R. S.
"Classification, cataloging, and care of sound recordings."
In *Classical Music Recordings for Home and Library* (Chicago: American Library Association, 1971); pp. 250-77.

503 Hambelton, W. A.
"Vital records protection."
Records Management Quarterly 3 (April 1969): 27-31.

504   Hamlin, A. T.
      "First considerations for the flood season: when catastrophe strikes, find an expert."
      Wilson Library Bulletin 48 (April 1974): 660-663.

505   Hamlin, A. T.
      "Florence flood."
      American Libraries 5 (November 1974): 525.
      (letter)

506   Hamlin, A. T.
      "The libraries of Florence, November 1966."
      ALA Bulletin 61 (February 1967): 141-51.

507   Hamlin, A. T.
      "Library crisis in Italy."
      Library Journal 92 (July 1967): 2516-22.
      (*See* B 3.11)

      Hanlan, J. F.
      See 601, Joel, A.

508   Hardesty, G. T.
      "Most neglected area."
      Library Scene 4 (September 1975): 24-26.
      Reprinted from *Library Binder* (May 1959).

509   Harding, E.
      "Further experience in the use of N-Methyl-2-Pyrrolidone as a solvent for old flour paste."
      The Paper Conservator 2 (1977): 6-8.

510   Harker, M. F.
      "Gelatin silver halide processes."
      In Royal Photographic Society of Great Britain, *The Recognition of Early Photographic Processes, Their Care and Conservation* (London: Royal Photographic Society of Great Britain, 1974).

511   Harley, R. D.
      Artists' Pigments c. 1600–1835: A Study in English Documentary Sources.
      New York: American Elsevier Publishing Company, 1970.

512 Harris, J. B.
"Practical aspects of lighting as related to conservation."
In Thomson, G., ed., *Contributions to the London Conference on Museum Climatology, 18-23 September 1967* (London: International Institute for Conservation of Historic and Artistic Works, 1968), pp. 133-38.

513 Harrison, H. P.
"Storage and preservation [of films]."
In Film Library Techniques: Principles of Administration (New York: Hastings House, 1973), pp. 177-92.

514 Harrop, D. A.
"Craft binders at work: Roger Powell."
Book Collector 22 (Winter 1973): 479-86.

515 Hartmann, G. J.
"Brandpreventie in bibliotheekmagazijnen" ("Fire prevention in library stack-rooms").
Open 2 (December 1970): 820-25.

516 Harvey, B. K.
"Fire hazards in libraries."
Library Security Newsletter 1 (January 1975): 1+; (March 1975): 1+; (May 1975): 9-10; (July 1975): 1+; (September 1975): 12-13; (November 1975): 10-11.

517 Harvey, B. K.
"Sprinkler systems and books."
Library Journal 99 (July 1974): 1741.
(letter)

518 Harvey, J.
"Air-conditioning for museums."
Museums Journal 73 (1973): 11-16.

Haslam, R.
See 470, Giles, C. H.

519 Hasznos, L.
"Modern methods for the protection of archival and library material."
Unesco Bulletin for Libraries 24 (November-December 1970): 302-304.

520   Hatton, M.
      "Enzymes in a viscous medium."
      The Paper Conservator 2 (1977): 9.

521   Hauser, R.
      "Examination: forms and methods."
      Bulletin of the American Institute for Conservation of Historic and Artistic Works 15, 1 (1974): 45-47.

522   Hauser, R.
      "Nondestructive examination of bookbindings: using radiography for documentation of a craft."
      Technology and Conservation 2 (Summer 1977): 34-36.

523   Hauser, R.
      Restoration Papers: A Survey of Papers Used by American Print and Book Conservators.
      North Andover, Massachusetts: Busyhaus, 1977.

524   Haverling, S.
      "Technical aspects of the preservation of archival (security) microfilm."
      Unesco Bulletin for Libraries 29 (March-April 1975): 68-74.
      (*See* C 1.3)

525   Hawken, W. R.
      Copying Methods Manual.
      Chicago: American Library Association, 1966.
      (Library Technology Program Publication no. 11)
      (*See* C 3.13)

526   Hawken, W. R.
      "Making big ones out of little ones: current trends in micrographics."
      Library Journal   102 (October 15, 1977): 2127-31.
      (*See* C 3.1)

527   Hawken, W. R.
      Photocopying From Bound Volumes; A Study of Machines, Methods, and Materials.

Chicago: American Library Association, 1962.
(Library Technology Program Publication No. 6)

528 Hawkes, C. V.
"Page adhesion and paper properties in unsewn binding."
Penrose Annual 65 (1972): 171-75.

529 Hayes, R. M., and J. Becker.
"Equipment for photographic files."
In *Handbook of Data Processing for Libraries* (New York: Wiley, 1970), pp. 379-97.

Hebert, R. L.
See 1342, Wilson, W. K.

530 Hegel, G. L.
"Equipment review: computer print out storage."
Records Management Quarterly 5 (January 1971): 42-43, 52-53.

531 Heller, J.
Printmaking Today; A Studio Handbook.
New York: Holt, Rinehart, and Winston, 1972.
2d ed.

532 Hemmerle, J.
"10 Jahre Sicherungsverfilmung: Ruckblick, Ergebnisse, Aufgaben" ("Ten years of preservation filming: review, results, lessons").
Der Archivar 24 (November 1971): cols. 357-64.
Abstract in *American Archivist* 36 (January 1973):100.

533 Henderson, J. W.
Memorandum on Conservation of the Collections.
New York: The New York Public Library, 1970.
(*See* A 2.5)

534 Henderson, J. W., and R. G. Krupp.
"The librarian as conservator."
Library Quarterly 40 (January 1970): 176-91.
(*See* A 3.5)

535   Henderson, W. T.
      "Binding—a librarian's view."
      In Allen, W. C., ed. *Serial Publications in Large Libraries*
      (Urbana: University of Illinois Graduate School of
      Library Science, 1970), pp. 95-107.
      (Allerton Park Institute, no. 16)
      (*See* D 4.5)

536   Hendrick, C., and M. E. Murfin.
      "Project library ripoff: a study of periodical mutilation
      in a university library."
      College and Research Libraries 35 (November 1974):
      402-11.
      (*See* B 4.7)

      Hendrick, C.
      See 821, Murfin, M. E.

537   Hentschel, R. A. A.
      "Paper-like products from synthetic polymers."
      Tappi 55 (1972): 1174-78.

538   Herf, E.
      "Neuere Massnahmen zur Aktualisierung des Berech-
      nungssystems von Buchbinderarbeiten" ("New mea-
      sures to bring up to date the system of calculation of
      bookbinding work").
      *Verband der Bibliotheken des Landes Nordrhein-
      Westfalen Mitteilungsblatt* 23 (September 1973):
      268-72.

539   Hey, M.
      "Kitchen chemistry: the reasons why not."
      The Abbey Newsletter, no. 11 (October 1977): 1-4.

540   Hey, M.
      "Paper bleaching: its simple chemistry and working
      procedures."
      The Paper Conservator 2 (1977): 10-23.

541 Hey, M.
"The use of the scanning electron microscope in document restoration problems."
Restaurator 1 (1970): 233-244.

542 Hey, M., and P. Waters.
"Heat set tissue."
Paper presented at the 5th annual meeting of the American Institute for Conservation of Historic and Artistic Works, May 30—June 2, 1977.

543 Hickman, T.
"Cloth case binding repair."
Private Library 7 (Summer 1966): 35-39.

544 Higham, R. R. A.
A Handbook of Paperboard and Board; Its Manufacturing Technology, Conversion and Usage.
London: Business Books, 1970-71.

545 Higham, R. R. A.
A Handbook of Papermaking; The Technology of Pulp, Paper, and Board Manufacture.
London: Business Books, 1968.
2d ed.

546 "Highsmith book repairs."
Unabashed Librarian 18 (Winter 1976): 10-13.

Hinkle, J.
See 274, Collier, V.

547 Hochfield, S.
"Conservation: the need is urgent."
Art News, February 1976, pp. 26-33.

Hockey, J. A.
See 379, Edwards, C. J.

548 Hoffberg, J. A.
"Ephemera in the art collection."
Library Trends 23 (January 1975): 483-93.

549   Hoffberg, J. A.
       "To preserve and to protect: a call to action."
       Special Libraries Association, Picture Division, *Picture-
       Scope* 19 (Summer 1971): 84-90.

550   Hoffman, A.
       "Preserving historical materials: recovering a region's
       heritage."
       Oklahoma Librarian 22 (October 1972): 7-8.

551   Holliday, C. A.
       "Problem of pages being cut out of library books to
       illustrate work that the children are doing for school."
       *Feliciter: Newsletter of the Canadian Library Associa-
       tion* 21 (April 1975): 14.
       (letter)

552   Holmes, D. C.
       *Determination of the Environmental Conditions in a
       Library for the Effective Utilization of Microforms.*
       Washington, D. C.: Association of Research Libraries,
       1970.

553   Holtman, E.
       "Security problem."
       Michigan Librarian 39 (Autumn 1973): 5-6.

554   Hopler, F. B.
       "Micrographics: processing, storage and protection."
       Records Management Quarterly 10 (April 1976):
       34-36.

555   Hoppe, R. A., and E. C. Simmel.
       "Book tearing and the bystander in the university
       library."
       College and Research Libraries 30 (May 1969): 247-51.
       (*See* B 4.11)

556   Horton, C.
       Cleaning and Preserving Bindings and Related Materials.
       Chicago: American Library Association, 1969.
       2d. ed. rev.

(Library Technology Program Publication No. 16)
(*See* D 1.10)

557 Horton, C.
"Conservation problems of Audubon's *Birds of America.*"
AIC Preprints (1977): 72-82.
(Paper presented at the 5th annual meeting of the American Institute for Conservation of Historic and Artistic Works)

558 Horton, C.
"The restoration of the Salisbury Bible."
Guild of Book Workers Journal 4, 2 (1966): 24-27.

559 Horton, C.
"Saving the libraries of Florence."
Wilson Library Bulletin 41 (June 1967): 1034-43.

Horton, C.
See 639, King, A.; 1293, Waters, P.

560 "How long will microfilm last?"
Kodak Panorama 5, 1 (1970): 2-3.

561 "How to examine bindings: a 10 point checklist."
Library Scene 5 (September 1976): 22-23.

562 Howorth, F. H.
"An approach to air conditioning."
In Thomson, G., ed., *Contributions to the London Conference on Museum Climatology, 18-23 September 1967* (London: International Institute for Conservation of Historic and Artistic Works, 1968).

Hoyer, H.
See 436, Flink, J.

563 Hubbard, L.
"Don't play hide and seek (cut up magazines instead)."
Unabashed Librarian 6 (Winter 1973): 16-17.

564   Hudson, F. L.
       "Acidity of seventeenth and eighteenth century books in two libraries."
       Paper Technology 8, 3 (1967): 189-90.

565   Hudson, F. L.
       "The sorption of sulphur dioxide through printing papers and their chemical resistance."
       Wochenblatt für Papierfabrikation 95 (1967): 660-663.

       Hudson, F. L.
       See 379, Edwards, C. J.

       Hueck-Van Der Plas, E. H.
       See 1283, Walters, A. H.

566   Humphries, P.
       An Investigation into the Physical Wear and Length of Life of Books for Young Children, 1967-1969.
       Birmingham: The Library Association, Youth Libraries Group, 1970.
       (LAYLG Pamphlet, no. 6)

567   Humphry, J. A.
       "Preservation and restoration of library materials."
       Rub-Off 20 (May 1969): 22-25.

568   Hunter, D.
       Papermaking; The History and Technique of an Ancient Craft.
       New York: Alfred A. Knopf, 1967.

569   Hurst, R. M.
       "Putting a collection on film."
       Curator 13 (1970): 199-203.

570   Hutcheon, N. B.
       "Fire protection in air system installations."
       Heating, Piping and Air-Conditioning 40, 12 (1968): 102-106.

I

571 "I danni subiti dagli archivi italiani nelle alluvioni del Novembre 1966" ("The damages suffered by the Italian archives in the floods of November 1966"). *Rassegna Degli Archivi di Stato* 26, 3 (1966): 345-564. Abstract in *American Archivist* 31 (October 1968): 404.

572 Ibrahim, K.
"Synthetic paper."
Reproduction Methods 10, 8 (1970): 27, 36.

Idelson, M.
See 1067, Rodgers, H. G.

573 Illuminating Engineering Society.
Lighting of Art Galleries and Museums.
London: Illuminating Engineering Society, 1970.
(IES technical report, no. 14)

574 Indictor, N., N. S. Baer, and W. H. Phelan.
"Evaluation of pastes for use in paper conservation."
Restaurator 2 (1975): 139-49.

Indictor, N.
See Baer, N. S.; 601, Joel, A.; 975, Phelan, W. H.

575 Ingram, V.
Conservation Manual.
Columbus, Ohio: Ohio Historical Society, 1976.

576 Ingram, V.
"Conservation of archives and library materials."
AIC Preprints (1977): 122-128.
(Paper presented at the 5th annual meeting of the American Institute for Conservation of Historic and Artistic Works)

577   "Ink drying: electronics promise basic changes."
        Book Production Industry 45, 4 (1969): 48-50.

578   "Inquiring archivist: heat-sensitive copy paper."
        Society of American Archivists Newsletter, March
        1977, p. 15.

        Institute of Paper Chemistry.
        See 592, Isenberg, I. H.

579   International Association of Music Libraries. Research
        Libraries Commission.
        Conservation in Music Libraries.
        London: International Association of Music Libraries,
        1977.
        (*See* A 2.1)

580   "International campaign for Florence and Venice."
        Unesco Courier 20 (January 1967).
        (special issue)

581   "International colloquium on the care and photographic
        reproduction of manuscripts and rare books."
        Herald of Library Science 15 (January 1976): 84-85.

        International Council of Museums. Committee for Museum
        Laboratories.
        See 291, Coremans, P.

582   International Council on Archives. Microfilm Committee.
        "Recommendations of the ICA Microfilm Committee:
        October 1974."
        Bulletin of the International Council on Archives 4
        (June 1975): 12-13.

        International Council on Archives.
        See 583, International Federation of Library Associa-
        tions.

        International Council on Archives.
        See Leisinger, A. H.

583 International Federation of Library Associations, and the International Council on Archives.
"Physical protection of books and documents; report of the joint consultation between the ICA and IFLA held in Paris, at the Unesco building on the 19th, 20th and 21st November 1973."
IFLA News 47 (February 1974): 16-18.

584 International Institute for Conservation of Historic and Artistic Works.
Conservation of Paintings and the Graphic Arts.
London: IIC, 1972.
(Preprints of contributions to the Lisbon conference, 1972)
(*See also* article from this work, cited separately, by C. Basile.)

585 International Institute for Conservation of Historic and Artistic Works.
Control of the Museum Environment: A Basic Summary.
London: IIC, 1967.

586 International Institute for Conservation of Historic and Artistic Works, American Group.
The Murray Pease Report; Code of Ethics for Art Conservators; Articles of Association of IIC; Bylaws of the American Group.
IIC–AG, 1968.

587 International Paper Company.
Pocket Pal: A Graphic Arts Digest for Printers and Advertising Production Managers.
New York: International Paper Company, 1970.
10th ed.

588 "Internationaler restauratorentag der arbeitsgemeinschaft der archiv-bibliothek und graphikrestauratoren, Freiburg-Br., Basel, Zurich, 4-9 settembre 1967" ("International restoration day of the work association of archive-library and graphic art restoration, Freiburg, Basel, Zurich, September 4-9, 1967").

Bollettino dell'Istituto di Patologia del Libro 26 (July-December 1967): 261-62.

589   "Inventor receives patent for casemaking process based on electronic heating."
Publishers' Weekly 208 (July 7, 1975): 67-68.

590   Irigoin, J.
"Conservateur en mission dans un ministère: métier d'hier et métier d'aujourd'hui."
Gazette des Archives 89 (1975): 75-81.

591   Irvine, B. J.
Slide Libraries: A Guide for Academic Institutions and Museums.
Littleton, Colorado: Libraries Unlimited, 1974.

592   Isenberg, I. H.
Pulp and Paper Microscopy.
Appleton, Wisconsin: Institute of Paper Chemistry, 1967.
3d ed.

593   Isom, W. R.
"How to prevent and cure record warping."
High Fidelity Magazine 22, 9 (1972): 50-53.

Institute of Paper Chemistry.
See 1298, Weiner, J.

594   Iusupova, M. V.
"Nekotorye voprosy stareniia i restarratsii kozhanykh perepletov knig" ("Some questions on the aging and restoration of leather bookbindings").
Sovetskoe Bibliotekovedenie 3 (1975): 112-116.

595   Izard, A. R.
"Children's books: comparative binding survey."
Unabashed Librarian 12 (Summer 1974): 19-25.

J

Jacobs, C.
See 245, Chatters, R. M.

596 James, A.
"Long-life paper and Winston's works."
Penrose Annual 68 (1975): 239-44.

James, T. H.
See 951, Ostroff, E.

597 Jedrzejewska, H.
Ethics in Conservation.
Stockholm: Kungl. Konsthögskolan, Institutet för materialkunskap, 1976.

598 Jenkins, J. F., ed.
Protecting our Heritage; a Discourse on Fire Protection and Prevention in Historic Buildings and Landmarks.
Boston: National Fire Protection Association, 1970.

599 "Jewish archive in Cambridge and its conservation."
Archives 11 (Spring 1974): 172-73.

600 " 'Jock the Ripper' is apprehended in South Dakota."
Library Journal 97 (September 1, 1972): 2680-81.

601 Joel, A., N. Indictor, J. F. Hanlan, and N. S. Baer.
"The measurement and significance of pH in paper conservation."
International Institute for Conservation of Historic and Artistic Works, Bulletin of the American Group 12, 2 (1972): 119-25.

Joel, A.
See 64, Baer, N. S.

602   Johnson, A. W.
      The Thames and Hudson Manual of Bookbinding.
      London: 1978.

603   Johnson, B. B., and T. Cairns.
      "Art conservation: culture under analysis."
      Analytical Chemistry 44, 1 (1972): 24A-36A; 44, 2
      (1972): 30A-38A.

      Jones, J. B.
      See 1163, Stevenson, A.; 1188, Tanselle, G. T.

604   Jones, M.
      "Guarding and filing—the assemblage and binding of
      miscellaneous documents."
      The Paper Conservator 2 (1977): 24-35.

605   Jones, M.
      "Seal repair, molds and casts."
      The Paper Conservator 1 (1976): 12-18.

606   Jonson, L. F.
      "Preservation of art for the art dealer and framer,
      part 1."
      Art Dealer and Framer, August 1976, pp. 14-15.
      (*See* D 5.5)

607   Jonson, L. F.
      "Paper deacidification, part 2."
      Art Dealer and Framer, October 1976, pp. 9-13.
      (*See* D 5.5)

      Jordan, A. T.
      See 244, Chandler, M.

608   Jordan, M.
      "Hurricane recovery efforts: University of Corpus
      Christi Library."
      Texas Library Journal 46 (Winter 1970): 210-13.

609   Jordan, R., and C. Blumenfeld.
       "The Jordan plastic book box: a new concept in library
       storage and circulation."
       Library Resources and Technical Services   12 (Fall
       1968): 435-41.

610   Jørgensen, H.
       "Aufbewahrung und Verzeichnung von älteren Karten
       und   Plänen   im   Seeländischen   Landesarchiv   in
       Kopenhagen"   ("Preservation and registration of old
       maps and charts in the Zealand national archives in
       Copenhagen").
       Der Archivar   24 (November 1971): cols. 389-96.

611   Judge, J.
       "Florence rises from the flood."
       National Geographic   132 (July 1967): 1-43.

612   Jullande, I.
       "Varför förstors papper och vad kan göras ât det"
       ("Why does paper deteriorate and what can one do
       about it").
       Biblioteksbladet 55, 7-8 (1970): 248-51.

613   Jütte, W.
       "Restaurierung und buchpflege an deutschen biblio-
       theken; analyse und gedanken zum ergebnis eines
       fragebogens"   ("Restoration and care of books at
       German libraries; analysis and thoughts on the result
       of a questionnaire").
       Zeitschrift für Bibliothekswesen und Bibliographie
       18, 3 (1971): 163-70.

K

614   Kaiser, F. E., ed.
       *Handling Special Materials in Libraries; A Project of the
       South Atlantic Chapter, SLA.*
       New York: Special Libraries Association, 1974.

615 Kalvar Corporation.
     Storage of Processed Kalvar Vesicular Film.
     New Orleans: Kalvar Corporation, n. d.
     (Technical sales bulletin)

616 "Kalvar reports progress in settling damage claims."
     Library Journal 98 (April 1, 1973): 1071-72.

617 "Kalvar wins government microfilm contract."
     American Libraries 4 (October 1973): 538-39.

618 Kane, L. M.
     A Guide to the Care and Administration of Manuscripts.
     Nashville: American Association for State and Local
     History, 1966.
     2d ed.
     (*See* E 3.10)

619 Kathpalia, Y. P.
     Conservation and Restoration of Archive Materials.
     Paris: Unesco, 1973.
     (Documentation, Libraries and Archives: Studies and
     Research, no. 3)
     (*See* E 3.5)

620 Kathpalia, Y. P.
     "The problem of acidity in the conservation of docu-
     ments."
     Unesco Bulletin for Libraries 29 (September-October
     1975): 268-270.

621 Kathpalia, Y. P.
     "Solvent lamination and 'India-7'."
     Indian Pulp and Paper 21 (1966): 323-25.

     Kathpalia, Y. P.
     See 90, Banks, P. N.

622 Katsarova, M.
     "Faktori za stareene na khartiiata i grizhi za opazvane
     na dokumentite" ("Factors affecting the aging of paper
     and efforts to preserve documents").
     Izvestiia na Durzhavnite Arkhivi 13 (1967): 129-37.
     Abstract in *American Archivist* 32 (January 1969): 41.

Katz, W. A.
See 1225, Trelles, O. M.

623 Kaula, P. N.
Library Buildings: Planning and Design.
New Delhi: Vikas Publications, 1971.

624 Keck, C. K.
"Can we afford to ignore facts?"
History News 30, 2 (February 1975): 34, 51.

625 Keck, C. K.
"The role of the conservator."
In Timmons, S., ed., *Preservation and Conservation:
Principles and Practices* (Washington, D. C.: National
Trust for Historic Preservation in the U. S., Preservation
Press, 1976), pp. 25-33.

626 Keck, C. K.
Safeguarding Your Collection in Travel.
Nashville: American Association for State and Local
History, 1970.

627 Keck, C. K., and others.
A Primer on Museum Security.
Cooperstown, New York: New York State Historical
Association, 1966.
(*See also* articles from this work, cited separately, by
N. Stolow.)

628 Keck, S.
"The life expectancy of materials and problems of
increasing visitor use."
In Timmons, S., ed., *Preservation and Conservation:
Principles and Practices* (Washington, D. C.: National
Trust for Historic Preservation in the U. S., Preservation
Press, 1976), pp. 327-39.

629 Keck, S.
"A little training can be a dangerous thing."
Museum News 52, 4 (1973): 40-42.

630   Kelly, G. B.
        "Practical aspects of deacidification."
        Bulletin of the American Institute for Conservation of Historic and Artistic Works   13, 1 (1972): 16-28.

631   Kelly, G. B., and J. C. Williams.
        "Mass deacidification with diethyl zinc, large-scale trials."
        AIC Preprints (1978): 81-92.
        (Paper presented at the 6th annual meeting of the American Institute for Conservation of Historic and Artistic Works)
        (*See* D 5.1)

632   Kelly, G. B., L. C. Tang, and M. K. Krasnow.
        "Methylmagnesium carbonate—an improved non-aqueous deacidification agent."
        In Williams, J. C., ed., *Preservation of Paper and Textiles of Historical and Artistic Value*
        (Washington, D. C.: American Chemical Society, 1977), pp. 62-71.
        (Advances in Chemistry Series, no. 164)
        (*See* D 5.2)

      Kelly, G. B.
        See 1334 and 1335, Williams, J. C.

633   Kent, G. O.
        "Copying of archives and foreign manuscript collections."
        In Perman, D. H., *Bibliography and the Historian; Conference at Belmont of the Joint Committee on Bibliographical Services to History, May 1967.*
        (Santa Barbara, California: CLIO 1968), pp. 103-108.

634   Kern, J.
        "Mr. fix-it: AV maintenance."
        Ohio Association of School Librarians Bulletin
        26 (January 1974): 48-49.

635 Kesler, E. G.
"A campaign against mutilation."
Journal of Academic Librarianship 3, 1 (March 1977):
29-30.
(*See* B 4.2)

636 Keyes, K. M.
"A manual method of paper pulp application in the
conservation of works of art on paper."
The Paper Conservator 1 (1976): 33-34.

637 Keyes, K. M., and D. S. Farnsworth.
"Practical applications of paper pulp in the conservation
of works of art on paper."
AIC Preprints (1976): 76-86.
(Paper presented at the 4th annual meeting of the
American Institute for Conservation of Historic and
Artistic Works)

638 King, A.
"Conservation of drawings and prints."
Special Libraries 63 (March 1972): 116-120.

639 King, A.
Review of C. Horton, *Cleaning and Preserving Books
and Related Materials*, 2d ed.
Studies in Conservation 17 (May 1972): 89.

640 King, A., A. Pelikan, and W. E. Falconer.
"The use of the archivist's pen and universal pH solution
for estimating the surface pH of paper."
Studies in Conservation 15 (1970): 63-64.

641 Kinney, J. M.
"Archival security and insecurity."
American Archivist 38 (October 1975): 493-97.

642 Kinney, J. M.
"Restoration of documents in the Texas State
Archives."
Texas Libraries 31 (Winter 1969): 146-49.

643 Kish, J.
"Latter-day view of vital records protection."
Office 67 (February 1968): 34-36.

644 Kish, J.
"Preparation of damaged forms for microfilming."
Data Systems News 9 (March 11, 1968): 20.

Kishore, R.
See 493 and 494, Gupta, R. C.

645 Klein, H.
"Microfilm resuscitation: a case study."
Journal of Micrographics 9 (July-August 1976): 299-303.
(*See* D 6.3)

646 Knightbridge, A. A. H.
"Sulphur dioxide test papers."
Journal of the Society of Archivists 4 (April 1970): 64-65.
(Notes and news)

647 Koefod, C. F.
"The handling and storage of computer tapes."
Data Processing 11 (July 1969): 20-23, 26-28.
(*See* D 6.9)

648 Koshofer, G.
"Thirty years of modern colour photography; 1935–1965."
British Journal of Photography 113 (1966): 562-63, 606-609, 644-49.

649 Kowalik, R.
Review of G. M. Cunha, *Conservation of Library Materials.*
Studies in Conservation 19 (February 1974): 58-63.

650 Kowalik, R., and I. Sadurska.
"Disinfection of infected stores or rooms in archives, libraries and museums."
Bollettino dell'Istituto di Patologia del Libro 24 (January-December 1965): 121-28.

Kowalik, R.
See 1076, Sadurska, I.

651   Kozocsa, I.
"Az egyházi könyvtárak muzeális értékeinek restaurálása" ("Restoration of precious materials of ecclesiastical libraries").
Magyar Könyvszemle 91, 2 (1975): 154-63.

652   Kozocsa, I.
"Restauro di monoscritti musicali del seicento e del settecento" ("Restoration of manuscripts on music from the 17th and 18th centuries").
Magyar Könyvszemle 88, 1-2 (1972): 27-31.

653   Kraan, B.
"Brand in archief of bibliotheek wordt vaak te laat ontdekt" ("Fire in the archive or library is often discovered too late").
Open 6 (January 1974): 10-14.

654   Kraemer Koeller, G.
Tratado de la previsión del papel y de la conservación de bibliotecas y archivos.
Madrid: Dirección General de Archivos y Bibliotecas, 1973.

Krasnow, M. K.
See 632, Kelly, G. B.

655   Kringstad, K.
"Degradation of wood and high-yield pulps by light."
Tappi 52 (1969): 1070-74.

Krupp, R. G.
See 534, Henderson, J. W.

656   Kubes, P.
"K problematice konzervace archivalii" ("A note on preservation of archival materials").
Archivni Časopis 20 (1970): 145-49.
Abstract in *American Archivist* 35 (July-October 1972): 430.

657   Kühn, H.
      "The use of heat-protection filters when works of art
      are filmed or televised."
      Studies in Conservation 12 (1967): 102-115.

658   Kühn, H.
      Wörterbuch der Handbuchbinderei und der Restaurie-
      rung von Einbanden, Papyri, Handschriften, Graphiken,
      Autographen, Urkunden, und Globen in deutscher,
      englisher, französischer, und italienisher Sprache
      ("Glossary for hand bookbinding and for the restoration
      of bindings, papyrus, manuscripts, graphic materials,
      autographs, documents, and globes in German, English,
      French, and Italian").
      Stuttgart: Hettler, 1969.

659   Kupferberg, A.
      "Archives."
      Films in Review 28 (January 1977): 53-55.

660   Kurth, W. H., and R. W. Grim.
      Moving a Library.
      New York: Scarecrow, 1966.
      (*See* B 2.11)

661   Kurttila, K. R.
      "Dry silver film stability."
      Journal of Micrographics 10 (January-February 1977):
      113-17.

662   Kusnerz, P. A.
      "Preservation of case photographs."
      Canadian Museum Association Gazette 7, 2 (1973).
      Reprinted from *Michigan Museums Review.*

663   Kusterer, J. E.
      "Permanence research at the W. J. Barrow Research
      Laboratory."
      In Cunha, G. M., and N. P. Tucker, eds., *Library and*
      Archives Conservation: The Boston Athenaeum's 1971
      Seminar on the Application of Chemical and Physical
      Methods to the Conservation of Library and Archival

Materials: May 17-21, 1971 (Boston: The Library of the Boston Athenaeum, 1972), pp. 77-88.

Kusterer, J. E.
See 358, Dupuis, R. N.

L

664 Labarre, A.
"Problèmes de la conservation" ("Conservation problems").
Association des Bibliothécaires Français Bulletin d'Informations 69 (1970): 257-62.

665 Ladenson, A.
"Library security and the law."
College and Research Libraries 38 (March 1977): 109-17.

666 Lafontaine, R. H.
Recommended Environmental Monitors for Museums, Archives and Art Galleries.
Ottawa: Canadian Conservation Institute, National Museums of Canada, 1975.
(Technical Bulletin no. 3)

667 LaHood, C. G.
"Microfilm for the Library of Congress."
College and Research Libraries 34 (July 1973): 291-94.

668 LaHood, C. G.
"Reproducing maps in libraries: the photographer's point of view."
Special Libraries 64 (January 1973): 19, 25-28.

669   LaHood, C. G., and R. C. Sullivan.
      Reprographic Services in Libraries: Organization and Administration.
      Chicago: American Library Association, 1975.
      (Library Technology Program Publication No. 19)
      (*See* C 3.4)

      LaHood, C. G.
      See 415, Finzi, J. C.

670   Lakhanpal, S. K.
      Library Binding Manual.
      Saskatoon: Serials Department, Murray Memorial Library, University of Saskatchewan, 1972.

671   Lal, A.
      "Deterioration of books."
      Indian Librarian 22 (September 1967): 96-98.

672   Lal, A.
      "Paper making and permanency."
      Indian Librarian 21 (December 1966): 146-48.

673   Lal, A.
      "Repair brittle books with polythene."
      Libri 25, 3 (1975): 227-229.

674   Lamb, D. M.
      Bindability of Paper with Adhesives.
      Clinton, Massachusetts: Colonial Press, 1970.

675   Lambert, M.
      "Journée d'étude du 16 mars consacrée aux problèmes de la conservation des documents" ("One-day workshop on March 16 devoted to the problems of preservation of documents").
      Association des Bibliothécaires Français Bulletin d'Informations 83 (1974): 83.

676   "Laminating and rebinding facilities."
      School Librarian 21 (September 1973): 219.

677   Landau, R. M.
       "Microfiche reader human factors."
       Journal of Micrographics   10 (May-June 1977): 219-27.

678   Landers, J. J.
       "Mending tape for maps."
       Special Libraries   61 (October 1970): 466.
       (letter)

679   Lane, A. H.
       "Reprints in the preservation picture, and a drift aside."
       Special Libraries   63 (July 1972): 305-09.
       (*See*   C 3.11)

680   Langmead, S., and M. Beckman.
       *New Library Design: Guide Lines to Planning Academic
       Library Buildings.*
       Tronto and New York: Wiley, 1970.

681   Langwell, W. H.
       "Accelerated ageing tests for paper."
       Journal of the Society of Archivists   3 (April 1967):
       245-48.

682   Langwell, W. H.
       "Measurement of the effects of air pollution on paper
       documents."
       Journal of the Society of Archivists   5 (October 1976):
       372-73.

683   Langwell, W. H.
       "Methods of deacidifying paper."
       Journal of the Society of Archivists 3 (April 1969):
       491-94.

684   Langwell, W. H.
       "Recent developments in Postlip lamination processes."
       Journal of the Society of Archivists 3 (October 1968):
       360-61.

685   Langwell, W. H.
       "Vapor phase deacidification of books and documents."
       American Archivist   29 (October 1966): 566-68.

686 Langwell, W. H.
"The vapour phase deacidification of books and documents."
Journal of the Society of Archivists 3 (April 1966): 137-38.

687 Langwell, W. H.
"Vapour-phase de-acidification: a recent development."
Journal of the Society of Archivists 4 (April 1973): 597-98.

688 Lawani, S. M.
"Storage and preservation of microfilm under tropical conditions."
Libri 18, 3-4 (1968): 182-90.

689 Leatherman, D. G.
"Experiments with interinstitutional cooperation."
Michigan Librarian 39 (Summer 1973): 8.

690 Lee, B. H.
"Theatrical visual arts ephemera: care and protection."
In Perry, T., ed., *Performing Arts Resources, Volume 1* (New York: Drama Book Specialists/Publishers, 1975), pp. 156-72.

691 Lee, M. M.
"Librarian as conservator."
Hawaii Library Association Journal 29, 1 (June 1972): 7-14.

692 Leene, J. E., ed.
Textile Conservation.
Washington, D. C.: Smithsonsian Institution, 1972.

693 Lehmann-Haupt, H., ed.
Bookbinding in America: Three Essays.
New York: R. R. Bowker, 1967.
Reprint of 1941 ed., rev. and with supplements.
(*See also* articles from this work, cited separately, by H. Lehmann-Haupt and J. W. Rogers.)

694 Lehmann-Haupt, H., ed.
"On the rebinding of old books."
In *Bookbinding in America: Three Essays.*
(New York: R. R. Bowker, 1967).
(*See* D 3.9)

695 Leisinger, A. H.
"International progress in microfilming: the background and work of the ICA Microfilm Committee."
American Archivist 39 (July 1976): 329-335.

696 Leisinger, A. H.
"More on permanence."
Microform Review 4 (April 1975): 91-99.
Reprinted from the International Council on Archives Microfilm Committee's *Bulletin* 3 (1974).

697 Leisinger, A. H.
Microphotography for Archives.
Washington, D. C.: International Council on Archives, 1968.

698 Leisinger, A. H.
Report of the Microfilming Committee.
Washington, D. C.: International Council on Archives, 1968.

699 Leisinger, A. H.
A study of the Basic Standards for Equipping, Maintaining, and Operating a Reprographic Laboratory in Archives.
Brussels: International Council on Archives, 1973.

700 Leisinger, A. H.
"User evaluation of microfilm readers for archival and manuscript materials; special report."
Microform Review 2 (July 1973): 177-209.

Lemcoe, M. M.
See 979, Pickett, A. G.

701   Lepeltier, R.
      Restauration des Dessins et Estampes.
      Paris: Societe Francaise du Livre, 1977.
      (Published English translation *The Restorer's Handbook
      of Drawings and Prints.* New York and London: Van
      Nostrand Reinhold, 1977)

702   Lerda, H.
      "Restauración de documentos; laminación y preser-
      vación" ("Restoration of documents; lamination and
      preservation").
      Revista del Archivo General de la Nacion 2, 2 (1972):
      59-68.

703   Levine, R. A.
      "How to protect your EDP records."
      New York Certified Public Accountant 39 (May 1969):
      353-56.

704   Lewis, F.
      "Paperback wearability."
      Library Journal 92 (June 1, 1967): 2096.
      (letter)

705   Lewis, J.
      "Requirements for an international center for preserva-
      tion of books and manuscripts."
      Bollettino dell'Istituto di Patologia del Libro 29 (Jan-
      uary-December 1970): 74-82.

706   Lewis, J.
      "Research on conservation of library materials."
      Archives 9 (October 1969): 161.

707   Lewis, R. H.
      Manual for Museums.
      Washington, D. C.: Department of the Interior, National
      Park Service, 1976.
      (*See* E 3.3)

708   "Libraries and vandalism: solutions sought."
      Library Journal 99 (May 1, 1974): 1252.

709 Library Association. Research and Development Committee.
The Care of Books and Documents.
London: Library Association, 1972.
(Library Association Research Publication, no. 10)
(*See* E 3.6)

Library Association of Australia.
See 102, Barnett, D.; 174, Boustead, W.; 1310, Wells, J. A.

710 Library Binding Institute.
Library Binding Institute Standard for Library Binding.
Boston: Library Binding Institute, 1971.
5th ed., rev.

Library Binding Institute.
See 1195, Tauber, M. F.

711 "Library consumer advocacy flares at Las Vegas."
American Libraries 4 (September 1973): 461.

712 Library of Congress.
Environmental Protection of Books and Related Materials.
Washington, D. C.: Library of Congress, 1975.
(Preservation Leaflet Series, no. 2)
(*See* B 2.4)

713 Library of Congress.
Marking Manuscripts.
Washington, D. C.: Library of Congress, 1977.
(Preservation Leaflet Series, no. 4)

714 Library of Congress.
Papermaking: Art and Craft; An Account Derived from the Exhibition Presented in the Library of Congress.
Washington, D. C.: Library of Congress, 1968.

715 Library of Congress.
Pre.serve.
Washington, D. C.: Library of Congress, ca. 1978.

716   Library of Congress.
        Preserving Leather Bookbindings.
        Washington, D. C.: Library of Congress, 1975.
        (Preservation Leaflet Series, no. 3)
        (*See* D 2.1)

717   Library of Congress.
        Preserving Newspapers and Newspaper-Type Materials.
        Washington, D. C.: Library of Congress, 1977.
        (Preservation Leaflet Series, no. 5)

718   Library of Congress.
        Proceedings of the Planning Conference for a National Preservation Program Held at the Library of Congress in Washington, D. C. on December 16 and 17, 1976.
        Washington, D. C.: Library of Congress, 1978.

719   Library of Congress.
        "Report on a planning conference for a national preservation program, Washington, D. C., December 16-17, 1976."
        Library of Congress Information Bulletin 36 (February 18, 1977): 129-31.
        (*See* A 4.2)

720   Library of Congress.
        Selected References in the Literature of Conservation.
        Washington, D. C.: Library of Congress, 1975.
        (Preservation Leaflet Series, no. 1)

721   Library of Congress. Photoduplication Service.
        "Permanence of library microforms; who is responsible? Recommendations for storage of permanent record microfilm."
        Microform Review 3 (October 1974): 248.
        (*See* C 1.4)

722   Library of Congress. Photoduplication Service.
        Specifications for the Microfilming of Books and Pamphlets in the Library of Congress.
        Washington, D. C.: Library of Congress, 1973.
        (*See* C 2.7)

723   Library of Congress. Photoduplication Service.
      Specifications for the Microfilming of Newspapers in the Library of Congress.
      Washington, D. C.: Library of Congress, 1972.
      (*See* C 2.8)

      Library of Congress. Preservation Office.
      See 1291, Waters, P.; 190, Brown, M.

724   "Library of Congress receives another patent; methylmagnesium carbonate as a non-aqueous deacidification agent."
      Library of Congress Information Bulletin 35 (March 12, 1976): 163-64.

725   "Library security: fire, bombs, water damage."
      Library Journal 102 (April 15, 1977): 857-58.

726   "Library security: mutilation, rape, vandals."
      Library Journal 100 (September 15, 1975): 1592.

727   "Life booster for paper."
      Chemical Week 98, 26 (June 25, 1966): 80.

728   "Light measurement."
      International Institute for Conservation of Historic and Artistic Works Newsletter 4, 4 (1967): 13.

729   Lightfoot, R. M.
      "Project mutilation: an attempt at a solution to a growing problem."
      Illinois Libraries 52 (November 1970): 946-49.
      (*See* B 4.10)

730   Limbacher, J. L.
      "Frightened of film fading? Beware the red menace."
      Film Library Quarterly 8, 1 (1975): 31.

731   Lindgren, E. H.
      "Preservation of cinematograph film in the national film archive."
      British Kinematography. Sound Telev. 5, 10 (1968): 290-92.

732 Line, M. B.
"Half-life of periodical literature: apparent and real obsolescence."
Journal of Documentation 26 (March 1970): 53-54.

733 Lisbeth, R. L.
"Paper shortage now a world problem."
Library of Congress Information Bulletin 33 (December 27, 1974): 423-424.

734 Litta, V.
"L'officina dei papiri ercolanesi di Napoli" ("Workshop for the papyrus of the ancient Ercolano in Naples").
Accademie e Biblioteche d'Italia 42 (January-April 1974): 28-32.

735 Lowe, D.
"The case of the vanishing records."
American Heritage 20, 5 (August 1969): 34-35, 107-111.

736 Lowry, B.
"Rescue; a report from Florence."
Arts Magazine 41 (Summer 1967): 44-46.

Luckmann, W.
See 785, Metcalf, R. L.

737 Luner, P.
"Paper permanence."
Tappi 52 (1969): 796-805.

738 Lusk, C. B.
"The invisible danger of visible light."
Museum News 53, 7 (1975): 22-23.

739 Lynden, F. C.
"Replacement of hard copy by microforms."
Microform Review 4 (January 1975): 15-24.
(*See* C 3.7)

M

MacClaren, R. H.
See 465, Gear, J. L.; 1343, Wilson, W. K.

740   Macleod, K. J.
         Museum Lighting.
         Ottawa: Canadian Conservation Institute, National
         Museums of Canada, 1975.
         (Technical Bulletin no. 2)

741   Macleod, K. J.
         Relative Humidity: Its Importance, Measurement and
         Control in Museums.
         Ottawa: Canadian Conservation Institute, National
         Museums of Canada, 1975.
         (Technical Bulletin no. 1)

742   Magarrell, J.
         "Damage in the stacks."
         Chronicle of Higher Education 41 (May 30, 1978):9.

743   Maheu, R.
         "International campaign for Florence and Venice; an
         appeal by the Director-General of Unesco."
         Feliciter; Newsletter of the Canadian Library Associa-
         tion 12 (December 1966–January/February 1967):
         37-38.

744   Maier, B. R.
         "In search of the perfect record cleanser."
         High Fidelity Magazine 22, 9 (1972): 52-55.

745   Majewski, L. J.
         "The education of art conservators."
         In Timmons, S., ed., *Preservation and Conservation:*
         Principles and Practices (Washington, D. C.: National
         Trust for Historic Preservation in the U. S., Preservation
         Press, 1976), pp. 481-92.

746 Majewski, L. J.
"On conservation."
Museum News 51, 9 (1973): 18-19.

747 Mark, H. F., S. M. Atlas, and E. Cernia, eds.
Man-Made Fibers; Science and Technology.
New York: Interscience Publishers, 1967-68.

748 Marriner, P. C.
"Criteria for packing works of art for travelling exhibitions."
Canadian Conservation Institute Newsletter 5 (1974): 3-5.

749 Martin, A. G.
Finishing Processes in Printing.
New York: Hastings House, 1972.

750 Martin, J. H.
"Restoring a flood damaged library."
Paper presented at Special Libraries Association conference, Chicago, June 1975.

751 Martin, J. H.
"Resuscitating a water-logged library."
Wilson Library Bulletin 50 (November 1975): 233-41.

752 Martin, R. G.
"Microforms and periodical mutilation."
Microform Review 2 (January 1973): 6-8.
(*See* B 4.8)

753 Martin, R. G.
"Mutilation: a college and university survey concerning microform replacement for mutilated periodicals and circulation of microforms."
Nebraska Library Association Quarterly 3 (Winter 1972): 18-20.

754 Martinique, E. G.
"Binding and preservation of Chinese double-leaved books."
Library Quarterly 43 (July 1973): 227-36.

755 Mason, D.
Document Reproduction in Libraries.
London: Association of Assistant Librarians, 1968.

Mason, L.
See 1104, Shapiro, C.

756 "Materials problems reviewed by Textbook Commission."
Publishers' Weekly 205 (April 1, 1974): 42.

757 Matthai, R. A.
"Energy conservation and management: a critical challenge for cultural institutions."
Technology and Conservation 3, 1 (Spring 1978): 12-20.

Matthews, D. A. R.
See 336, Davison, P. S.

758 Matthews, R. C.
"Book materials, manufacturing capacity may be scarce again by summer."
Publishers' Weekly 207 (April 7, 1975): 38-40.

759 Matthews, R. C.
" 'Greed and mismanagement' caused the recent shortages [of paper] ."
Publishers' Weekly 206 (December 2, 1974): 26.

760 Mattison, L.
"Worn book checklist for academic libraries."
Library Resources and Technical Services 14 (Fall 1970): 559-61.

761 Mauck, V. L.
"Selection and purchase of archival equipment and supplies."
Illinois Libraries 53 (January 1971): 18-21.

762 Maxin, J. A.
"Open shelving of journals on microfilm."
Special Libraries 66 (December 1975): 592-94.

763   Maxwell, M.
      "One great collector teaches another: what makes a 'rare book'?"
      Wilson Library Bulletin 48 (November 1973): 255-56.

764   Mayer, R.
      A Dictionary of Art Terms and Techniques.
      New York: Thomas Y. Crowell, 1969.

765   Mayer, R.
      "Technical page: permanent paper."
      American Artist 33 (February 1974): 10.

766   Mazal, O.
      "Probleme der aufbewahrung und restaurierung des Robert Musil Nachlasses" ("Problems of storage and restoration of the Robert Musil bequest").
      Biblos 23, 2 (1974): 119-129.

767   McCabe, R. F.
      "A base materials supplier talks about the history and growth of type II nonwoven book cover materials."
      Book Production Industry 50, 4 (1974): 15-19, 40.

768   McCarthy, P.
      "Vapor phase deacidification: a new preservation method."
      American Archivist 32 (October 1969): 333-342.

McComb, R.
      See 1293, Waters, P.

McCrea, J. L.
      See 8, Adelstein, P. Z.

769   McCrone, Walter C., Associates, Inc.
      Chemical Analytical Study of the Vinland Map; Report to the Yale University Library.
      Chicago: Walter C. McCrone Associates, 1974.

770 McDermott, J. C.
"Unique applications: critical material storage facilities."
Journal of Micrographics 11 (January-February 1978): 165-68.
(*See* C 1.1)

771 "McGraw-Hill shifts to use of permanent paper."
Publishers' Weekly 194 (July 1, 1968): 85-86.

772 McGregor, L., and J. Bruce.
"Recovery of flood damaged documents by the Queensland State Archives."
Archives and Manuscripts 5 (August 1974): 193-99.

773 McGuirl, M. C.
"Guarding against disaster."
Library of Congress Information Bulletin 32 (August 10, 1973): 146-47.

774 McKenna, D.
"Valley Bank recalls Teton Dam disaster; emergency recovery actions."
Journal of Micrographics 11 (November-December 1977): 137-39.

775 McKeon, D. B., and J. C. Gardner.
"Louisiana's drying documents."
Louisiana Library Association Bulletin 37 (Summer 1974): 43-47.

McKiel, M.
See 465, Gear, J. L.; 1343, Wilson, W. K.

776 McLean, R.
Victorian Publishers' Book-Bindings in Cloth and Leather.
London: Gordon Fraser, 1974.

McWilliams, L.
See 190, Brown, M.

Meckler, A. M.
See 1261 and 1262, Veaner, A. B.

777   Mehra, C. P.
      Art and Science of Book Preservation.
      Poona, India: Swaraj Publications, 1977.

778   Mehra, C. P.
      "Conservation of photographic archives."
      Conservation of Cultural Property in India 6 (1973):
      64-76.
      (*See* D 6.5)

779   Meister, H. J.
      "Zu einigen fragen der sicherung von bibliotheksbes-
      tänden" ("On some questions in safeguarding the
      bookstock").
      Zentralblatt für Bibliothekswesen 83 (April 1969):
      193-204.

780   Melot, M.
      "La restauration des livres et des estampes au Japon"
      ("Restoring books and prints in Japan").
      Bulletin des Bibliothèques de France 15 (January
      1970): 27-29.

781   Meneray, W. E.
      Tulane University Disaster Plan.
      New Orleans: Research and Publication Committee of
      the Library Department, 1977.
      (*See* B 3.4)

782   Menkus, B.
      "Reassessing vital records protection."
      Business Graphics 3, 12 (December 1969): 30-31.

783   Metcalf, K. D.
      "The design of book stacks and the preservation of
      books."
      Restaurator 1 (1969): 115-25.
      (*See* B 2.7)

784   Metcalf, K. D.
      Library Lighting.
      Washington, D. C.: Association of Research Libraries,
      1970.

785   Metcalf, R. L., and W. Luckmann, eds.
      Introduction to Insect Pest Management.
      New York: Wiley and Sons, 1975.

786   Meyers, S. K.
      "Saving the past for the future."
      Pennsylvania Library Association Bulletin 32 (September 1977): 101-102.

787   Michaels, P. E.
      "Accreditation, certification, and licensing of art conservators."
      In Timmons, S., ed., *Preservation and Conservation: Principles and Practices* (Washington, D. C.: National Trust for Historic Preservation in the U. S., Preservation Press, 1976), pp. 435-42.

788   Michelmore, D., and D. G. Vaisey.
      "Society of Archivists conservation conferences 1977 and 1978."
      The Paper Conservator 2 (1977): 51.

789   "Microfilm deterioration traced to paper boxes."
      Library Journal 95 (May 15, 1970): 1796.

790   "Microfilm in an uncertain world."
      Records Management Quarterly 1 (July 1967): 12-15.

791   "Microform reader/printer for libraries: a survey."
      Library Technology Reports, July 1972.
      (Microforms and equipment)

792   "Microform reader/printer product evaluations."
      Library Technology Reports, 1965- .

793   Middleton, B. C.
      "Book preservation and the librarian."
      In Williams, J. C., ed., *Preservation of Paper and Textiles of Historical and Artistic Value* (Washington, D. C.: American Chemical Society, 1977), pp. 3-23.
      (Advances in Chemistry Series, no. 164)

794 Middleton, B. C.
"Facsimile printing."
The Paper Conservator 1 (1976): 19-21.

795 Middleton, B. C.
The Restoration of Leather Bindings.
Chicago: American Library Association, 1972.
(Library Technology Program Publication No. 18)
(*See* D 2.4)

796 "Military records get freeze-dried."
Business Week September 22, 1973, p. 25.

797 "Millions of records saved by freeze drying process."
Library Journal 98 (December 1, 1973): 3491.

798 Mills, J. F.
"Problems and solutions."
Connoisseur 168 (August 1968): 251.

799 Mitra, D. K.
"Maps in libraries: their storage and preservation."
Herald of Library Science 7 (January 1968): 27-32.

800 Montana, J. A.
"Evaluating security equipment."
Administrative Management 28 (April 1967): 66-73.

801 Montuori, T. R.
"Testing recently processed microfilm for archival stability."
Journal of Micrographics 8 (November-December 1974): 79-82.

802 Montouri, T. R.
"Testing the archival stability of microfilm."
Office 83 (April 1976): 124.

803 Moon, M. J.
"Automation in bindery preparations."
Library Scene 3 (September 1974): 12-13.

804 Moor, I.
"The ambrotype: research into its restoration and conservation."
The Paper Conservator 1 (1976): 22-25.

805 Moor, I.
"The ambrotype: research into its restoration and conservation; part 2."
The Paper Conservator 2 (1977): 36-43.

806 Moran, R. F., Jr.
"Moving a large library."
Special Libraries 63 (April 1972): 163-72.

807 "More flood damage counsel from Cornell librarian."
Library Journal 97 (December 1, 1972): 3837.

808 Morgan, M.
"Saving a book cathedral from pollution."
Wilson Library Bulletin 48 (April 1974): 666-667.

809 Morris, J.
Managing the Library Fire Risk.
Berkeley: University of California Office of Insurance and Risk Management, 1975.
(*See* B 3.5)

810 Morrison, R. C.
"Experience in restoration; a workshop seminar conducted by the New England Document Conservation Center."
Library Scene 5 (June 1976): 30-31.
(*See* A 3.3)

811 Morrison, R. C.
"Improving library conservation."
Library Security Newsletter 2 (Spring 1976): 8-10.

812 Morrison, R. C., G. M. Cunha, and N. P. Tucker, eds.
Conservation Administration; Seminar on the Theoretical Aspects of the Conservation of Library and Archival Materials and the Establishment of Conservation

Programs, North Andover, Massachusetts, 1973.
North Andover, Massachusetts: New England Document
Conservation Center and the Library of the Boston
Athenaeum, 1975.
(*See also* articles from this work, cited separately, by
D. J. Fischer and R. Shoulberg.)

813   Mortimer, E. A.
      *Library Books: Their Care and Repair; A Handbook for
      Library Binding Instructors and Librarians.*
      Auckland, New Zealand: University of Auckland, 1968.

814   Mortimer, R.
      "Some warnings about 'Kitchen Chemistry'."
      AB Bookman's Weekly 60 (October 3, 1977): 1707-16.

815   Motta, E.
      O papel: problemas de conservacão e restauracão.
      Petropolis: Museu de Armas Ferreira da Cunha, 1971.

816   Mucci, P.
      Letter to the editor on health hazards in the use of non-
      aqueous methylmagnesium carbonate deacidification
      processes.
      Paper Conservation News, no. 6 (March 1976): 4.

817   Mucci, P.
      "Neutralizing and buffering book and manuscript paper:
      a guide to the magnesium bicarbonate process."
      Mid-Atlantic Archivist 4, 1 (January 1975): 3-8.

818   Muir, D.
      Binding and Repairing Books by Hand.
      New York: Arco, 1978.

819   Müller, G.
      "Die originalgetreue restaurierung wertvoller biblio-
      theksbestände auf der grandlage des Jenaer papiers-
      paltverfahrens" ("Restoration of valuable library mate-
      rials to their original condition using the Jena paper-
      splitting technique").
      Zentralblatt für Bibliothekswesen 84 (November 1970):
      641-658.

820 Müller, G.
"Zur problematik der restaurierung und konservierung wertvoller bücher und dokumente auf papiergrundlage" ("On the problem of restoration and conservation of valuable books and documents on paper").
Zentralblatt für Bibliothekswesen 83 (May 1969): 301-308.

Müller, G.
See 1235, Tröger, R.

821 Murfin, M. E., and C. Hendrick.
"Ripoffs tell their story: interviews with mutilators in a university library."
Journal of Academic Librarianship 1, 2 (May 1975): 8-12.
(*See* B 4.6)

Murfin, M. E.
See 536, Hendrick, C.

N

822 Napier, P. A.
"Developments in copying, micrographics, and graphic communication, 1975."
Library Resources and Technical Services 20 (Summer 1976): 236-58.

823 Napier, P. A.
"Developments in copying, micrographics, and graphic communications, 1976."
Library Resources and Technical Services 21 (Summer 1977): 187-215.
(*See* C 3.2)

824   National Archives and Records Service.
"Care of microfilm and microfilm readers."
American Archivist 37 (April 1974): 314-15.
(Technical notes)
(*See* C 1.5)

825   National Archives and Records Service.
Handbook for Recommended Environmental Conditions and Handling Procedures for Magnetic Tape.
Washington, D. C.: National Archives and Records Service, July 1972.
(draft version)

National Archives and Records Service.
See 335, Davis, L. E.

826   National Archives and Records Service. Office of Federal Records Centers.
Federal Records Centers; A GSA Handbook.
Washington, D. C.: National Archives and Records Service, 1967.
(Records management handbook)

827   National Archives and Records Service. Office of Records Management.
Microfilming Records.
Washington, D. C.: General Services Administration, National Archives and Records Services, Office of Records Management, 1974.
(*See* C 2.4)

828   National Archives and Records Service. Office of Records Management.
Microform Retrieval Equipment Guide, 1974.
Washington, D. C.: General Services Administration, National Archives and Records Service, Office of Records Management, 1975.

829   National Bureau of Standards.
Care of Books, Documents, Prints and Films.
Washington, D. C.: Government Printing Office, 1971.

National Bureau of Standards.
See 1341, Wilson, W. K.

830 "National Bureau of Standards finds causes of paper deterioration."
Technical News Bulletin of the National Bureau of Standards. 57, 7 (July 1973): 174.

National Central Library of Florence.
See 145, Biblioteca Nazionale Centrale di Firenza.

831 National Conservation Advisory Council.
Conservation of Cultural Property in the United States.
Washington, D. C.: NCAC, 1976.
(*See* A 4.5)

832 National Conservation Advisory Council.
Report from the Regional Centers Study Committee to the National Conservation Advisory Council.
Washington, D. C.: NCAC, 1976.
(*See* A 4.6)

833 National Conservation Advisory Council.
Report of the Study Committee on Libraries and Archives: National Needs in Library and Archives Conservation.
Washington, D. C.: NCAC, 1978.

834 National Conservation Advisory Council.
Statement on the Control of Environmental Conditions for Preservation of Cultural Property in Situations of Energy Shortage.
Washington, D. C.: NCAC, 1977.
Also published in *Special Libraries* 68 (November 1977): 419-20, and in *Society of American Archivists Newsletter,* September 1977, pp. 12-13.
(*See* B 2.1)

835 "National Endowment for the Humanities (NEH) has joined the Council on Library Resources (CLR) in awarding matching funds totaling $176,000 to Barrow Preservation Research, Inc."
College and Research Libraries News 5 (May 1976): 119.

836   National Fire Protection Association.
      Care and Maintenance of Sprinkler Systems.
      Boston: National Fire Protection Association, 1971.
      (NFPA, no. 13A)

837   National Fire Protection Association.
      "History, value and performance records of sprinklers."
      In *Fire Protection Handbook* (Boston: National Fire
      Protection Association, 1969), 13th rev. ed.

838   National Fire Protection Association.
      *Manual for Fire Protection for Archives and Record
      Centers.*
      Boston: National Fire Protection Association, 1972.

839   National Fire Protection Association.
      Protection of Library Collections.
      Boston: National Fire Protection Association, 1970.
      (NFPA, no. 910)

840   National Fire Protection Association.
      *Recommended Practice for Protection of Library Col-
      lections from Fire.*
      Boston: National Fire Protection Association, 1970.
      (NFPA, no. 910)

841   National Fire Protection Association.
      Standard for Foam Extinguishing Systems.
      Boston: National Fire Protection Association, 1970.
      (NFPA, no. 11)

842   National Fire Protection Association.
      Standard for the Installation of Sprinkler Systems.
      Boston: National Fire Protection Association, 1969.
      (NFPA, no. 13)

843   National Fire Protection Association.
      *Standard for the Storage and Handling of Cellulose
      Nitrate Motion Picture Film.*
      Boston: National Fire Protection Association, 1967.

844 National Fire Protection Association.
Standard on Carbon Dioxide Extinguishing Systems.
Boston: National Fire Protection Association, 1968.

845 National Fire Protection Association.
Standard on Halogenated Fire Extinguishing Agent Systems—Halon 1301.
Boston: National Fire Protection Association, 1971.

846 National Fire Protection Association. Committee on Libraries, Museums, and Historic Buildings.
Recommended Practice for Protection of Museum Collections from Fire.
Boston: National Fire Protection Association, 1969. (NFPA, no. 911)

National Fire Protection Association. Committee on Libraries, Museums, and Historic Buildings.
See 598, Jenkins, J. F.

847 National Fire Protection Association. Committee on Protection of Records.
Protection of Records, 1970.
Boston: National Fire Protection Association, 1970. (NFPA, no 232)

848 National Microfilm Association.
Bibliography of Micrographics.
Silver Spring, Maryland: National Microfilm Association, 1974.

849 National Microfilm Association.
Introduction to Micrographics.
Silver Spring, Maryland: National Microfilm Association, 1973.

850 National Microfilm Association.
List of Micrographic Standards and Related Terms.
Silver Spring, Maryland: National Microfilm Association, 1974.

851   National Microfilm Association.
       NMA Standard Inspection and Quality Control of First
       Generation Silver Halide Microfilm.
       Silver Spring, Maryland: National Microfilm Associa-
       tion, 1972.

852   National Microfilm Association.
       Standards.
       Silver Spring, Maryland: National Microfilm Associa-
       tion, 1972- .

       National Microfilm Association.
       See Avedon, D. M.

853   National Micrographics Association.
       Basic U. S. Micrographic Standards and Specifications.
       Silver   Spring,   Maryland: National   Micrographics
       Association, 1976.
       (*See* C 2.2)

854   National Micrographics Association.
       Buyer's Guide to Microfilm Equipment, Products, and
       Services.
       Silver   Spring,   Maryland: National   Micrographics
       Association, 1971- .

855   "National preservation program, first phase."
       Library of Congress Information Bulletin   26 (Jan-
       uary 26, 1967): 67-68.

856   Neilson, G.
       "New fire protection for high value areas."
       DuPont Magazine, January-February 1971.

857   "Negative transfer."
       Technical Photography   9, 2 (February 1977): 39.

858   Nelson, C. E.
       "The evolution of NMA standards work."
       Journal of Micrographics 9 (May-June 1976): 223-34.

859   Nelson, C. W.
        "Archival paper: a new archival bond paper released by
        Xerox."
        American Archivist 38 (October 1975): 575-76.
        (Technical notes)

860   Nelson, C. W.
        "Archival preservation."
        Drexel Library Quarterly   11 (January 1975): 87-96.

861   Nelson, C. W.
        "Archival quality of tape."
        American Archivist 37 (January 1974): 104.
        (Technical notes)

862   Nelson, C. W.
        "Cause and prevention of microfilm blemishes."
        American Archivist 33 (July 1970): 350-52.
        (Technical notes)

863   Nelson, C. W.
        "Color photography colloquium: first Colloquium on
        the collection and preservation of color photographs,
        1975."
        American Archivist 39 (April 1976): 228-29.
        (Technical notes)

864   Nelson, C. W.
        "Deterioration and preservation conference."
        American Archivist   33 (January 1970): 107-109.
        (Technical notes)

865   Nelson, C. W.
        "Emergency measures for water damage."
        American Archivist 36 (January 1973): 85-86.
        (Technical notes)

866   Nelson, C. W.
        "Federal microfilm regulations."
        American Archivist   35 (July-October 1972): 447-49.
        (Technical notes)

867   Nelson, C. W.
          "Fire prevention."
          American Archivist 36 (July 1973): 427-28.
          (Technical notes)

868   Nelson, C. W.
          "Fire protection consultant."
          American Archivist 34 (July 1971): 334.
          (Technical notes)

869   Nelson, C. W.
          "Foam fire control of records."
          American Archivist 29 (October 1966): 563.
          (Technical notes)

870   Nelson, C. W.
          "Freeze-dried documents."
          American Archivist 35 (July-October 1972): 443-44.
          Also published in *Chemistry* 45 (March 1972): 24.

871   Nelson, C. W.
          "Fumigation equipment."
          American Archivist 34 (July 1971): 336.
          (Technical notes)

872   Nelson, C. W.
          "Hollinger box test."
          American Archivist 30 (April 1967): 377-78.
          (Technical notes)

873   Nelson, C. W.
          "Hurricane Agnes flood report."
          American Archivist 37 (April 1974): 311.
          (Technical notes)

874   Nelson, C. W.
          "Hypo wash indicator."
          American Archivist 33 (January 1970): 105.
          (Technical notes)

875   Nelson, C. W.
         "Inexpensive document fumigator."
         American Archivist 36 (January 1973): 82-84.
         (Technical notes)

876   Nelson, C. W.
         "Library of Congress preservation activities."
         American Archivist 38 (October 1975): 576.
         (Technical notes)

877   Nelson, C. W.
         "Massachusetts conservation project."
         American Archivist 38 (April 1975): 221-22.
         (Technical notes)

878   Nelson, C. W.
         "Maximum safe pH."
         American Archivist 38 (January 1975): 65-66.
         (Technical notes)

879   Nelson, C. W.
         "McGraw-Hill permanent paper statement."
         American Archivist 31 (July 1968): 316-17.
         (Technical notes)

880   Nelson, C. W.
         "Microfilm storage containers."
         American Archivist 34 (October 1971): 404.
         (Technical notes)

881   Nelson, C. W.
         "Micrographics quality-control service."
         American Archivist 37 (January 1974): 99-100.
         (Technical notes)

882   Nelson, C. W.
         "Motion picture restoration printer."
         American Archivist 30 (October 1967): 614.
         (Technical notes)

883   Nelson, C. W.
         "National fire codes."
         American Archivist 37 (April 1974): 315.
         (Technical notes)

884   Nelson, C. W.
         "New archival box."
         American Archivist 36 (April 1973): 259.
         (Technical notes)

885   Nelson, C. W.
         "New computer fire standard."
         American Archivist 32 (January 1969): 97-98.
         (Technical notes)

886   Nelson, C. W.
         "New deacidification patent."
         American Archivist 39 (April 1976): 228.
         (Technical notes)

887   Nelson, C. W.
         "New display container."
         American Archivist 35 (April 1972): 237.
         (Technical notes)

888   Nelson, C. W.
         "New England Document Conservation Center."
         American Archivist 36 (April 1973): 257-58.
         (Technical notes)

889   Nelson, C. W.
         "New England Document Conservation Center."
         American Archivist 36 (July 1973): 425-26.
         (Technical notes)

890   Nelson, C. W.
         "New microfilm container."
         American Archivist 37 (January 1974): 101.
         (Technical notes)

891 Nelson, C. W.
"Newspaper copier."
American Archivist 38 (October 1975): 578-79.
(Technical notes)

892 Nelson, C. W.
"Neutron activation of faded photographs and documents."
American Archivist 32 (July 1969): 285-86.
(Technical notes)

893 Nelson, C. W.
"Nonaqueous deacidification solution."
American Archivist 37 (October 1974): 607-608.
(Technical notes)

894 Nelson, C. W.
"Nonaqueous spray deacidification."
American Archivist 36 (October 1973): 575-77.
(Technical notes)

895 Nelson, C. W.
"Ohio conservation grant."
American Archivist 37 (July 1974): 477.
(Technical notes)

896 Nelson, C. W.
"Paper clip investigation."
American Archivist 32 (July 1969): 289-90.
(Technical notes)

897 Nelson, C. W.
"Paper permanence."
American Archivist 30 (October 1967): 612-13.
(Technical notes)

898 Nelson, C. W.
"Paper shortage."
American Archivist 36 (July 1973): 430-31.
(Technical notes)

899   Nelson, C. W.
         "Paper shortage continues."
         American Archivist 37 (January 1974): 98-99.
         (Technical notes)

900   Nelson, C. W.
         "Permanence of Estar polyester base films."
         American Archivist 29 (July 1966): 428-29.
         (Technical notes)

901   Nelson, C. W.
         "Photo paper warning."
         American Archivist 39 (April 1976): 227.
         (Technical notes)

902   Nelson, C. W.
         "Reactor restores photographs."
         American Archivist 29 (April 1966): 297.
         (Technical notes)

903   Nelson, C. W.
         "Recycled paper."
         American Archivist   35 (July-October 1972): 444-45.
         (Technical notes)

904   Nelson, C. W.
         "Solution for newsprint shortage."
         American Archivist 37 (January 1974): 99.
         (Technical notes)

905   Nelson, C. W.
         "Standard on photo plate storage."
         American Archivist 36 (July 1973): 429-30.
         (Technical notes)

906   Nelson, C. W.
         "Surface pH determinations of paper."
         American Archivist 37 (July 1974): 475-77.
         (Technical notes)

907 Nelson, C. W.
       "Test of Xerox micro spheres paper."
       American Archivist 37 (April 1974): 313.
       (Technical notes)

908 Nelson, C. W.
       "World's largest warehouse."
       American Archivist 37 (January 1974): 103-104.
       (Technical notes)

909 Nelson, E. R.
       "Do we understand museum air conditioning?"
       Curator 11 (1968): 127-36.
       (*See* B 2.10)

910 Nelson, H. E.
       "Fire protection for archives and records centers."
       Records Management Quarterly 2 (January 1968): 19-23.

911 Nelson, H. E.
       "Protection and storage of EDP tapes."
       Records Management Journal 4, 4 (Winter 1966): 15-17.

912 Neufeld, J.
       "S-O-B: save our books."
       RQ 6 (Fall 1966): 25-28.

913 "New England Document Conservation Center."
       Unesco Bulletin for Libraries 28 (November-December 1974): 343.

914 "New England Document Conservation Center: disaster recovery units."
       Bookmark 33 (November 1973): 40.
       Also published in *NYLA Bulletin* 21 (December 1973): 3 and in *Vermont Libraries* 3 (January 1974): 4.

       New England Document Conservation Center.
       See Cunha, G. M. and R. C. Morrison.

915   New, P. G.
       Reprography for Librarians.
       London: Clive Bingley, 1975.

916   "New paper shortages may lie ahead."
       Publishers' Weekly 207 (May 5, 1975): 82-83.

917   "New photo conservation center."
       Library Journal 100 (September 15, 1975): 1593.

918   "New programme for archives preservation continues the
       work of Unesco's mobile microfilm units."
       Bibliography, Documentation, Terminology 10 (March
       1970): 48-49.

919   "New technique kills insect harmful to books."
       AB Bookman's Weekly 61 (January 9, 1978): 158-59.

920   New York Public Library.
       Report 1976/77
       New York: New York Public Library, 1977.
       (*See* A 5.1)

921   "*New York Times* claims Kalvar to satisfy library com-
       plaints."
       American Libraries 4 (July 1973): 409.

922   Newman, J. J.
       *Administrator's Manual: Preservation/Restoration of
       Documentary Materials.*
       Vincennes, Indiana: Society of Indiana Archivists, 1975.

923   Nichols, H.
       "Care and preservation of maps."
       In *Map Librarianship* (Bingley, Colorado: Shoe String
       Press, 1976), pp. 272-77.

924   Nichols, H.
       "Storage [of maps]."
       In *Map Librarianship* (Bingley, Colorado: Shoe String
       Press, 1976), pp. 112-33.

925   Nicol, J.
      "About old newspapers."
      Feliciter; Newsletter of the Canadian Library Association 20 (November 1974): 20.

926   Nielsen, T. F.
      "Restoration of a grants and leases register in the State Library of N.S.W."
      Archives and Manuscripts 6 (August 1975): 137-41.

927   Njuksha, J. P.
      "Problemy konservatsii i restauratsii bibliotechnykh fondov" ("Problems of preservation and restoration of library collections").
      Sovetskoe Bibliotekovedenie 3 (1975): 107-112.

928   Njuksha, J. P.
      "Technology of conservation and restoration of library materials."
      Restaurator 2 (1975): 65-79.

929   Nitecki, J. Z., ed.
      Directory of Library Reprographic Services.
      Weston, Connecticut: Microform Review, 1973.
      5th ed.
      (Sponsored by the Reproduction of Library Materials Section of RTSD/ALA)

930   "No relief in sight for the paper shortage."
      Publishers' Weekly 205 (January 28, 1974): 235.

931   "Non-silver film recommendation."
      Microform Review 4 (October 1975): 247.
      Also published in *Library Resources and Technical Services* 19 (Fall 1975): 413 and in *School Media Quarterly* 4 (Winter 1976): 400-401.

932   Noonan, C.
      "Solving a humidity control problem."
      Canadian Museums Association Gazette 8, 2 (Spring 1975): 21-25.

933 Nordstrand, O. K.
"Chinese double-leaved books and their restoration."
Libri 17, 2 (1967): 104-130.

934 Nordstrand, O. K.
"The conference on the international cooperation for the preservation of the book, Florence, March 12-14, 1970."
Restaurator 1 (1970): 214-20.
(*See* A 4.10)

935 Nordstrand, O. K.
"The future organization of conservation and restoration in Denmark."
Libri 20, 1-2 (1970): 101-104.

936 "Numero speciale dedicato a la cooperazione internazionale per la conservazione del libro; incontro di studi organizzato dalla Biblioteca Nazionale Centrale di Firenze, sooto gli auspici dell'Unesco e del Ministero della publica istruzione" ("Special issue dedicated to international cooperation in book conservation; study session organized by the National Central Library of Florence under the auspices of Unesco and the Ministry of Public Education").
Bollettino dell'Istituto di Patologia del Libro 29 (January-December 1970): 3-198.

937 "Nuovi laboratori di restauro a Firenze" ("New restoration laboratories in Florence").
Bollettino dell'Istituto di Patologia del Libro 28 (July-December 1969): 229-230.

O

O'Connell, M. R.
See 1031, Rath, F. L.

938 Oddy, W. A.
"An unsuspected danger in display."
Museums Journal 73 (1973): 27-28.
(*See* B 5.4)

939 Oddy, W. A., and C. J. Wheatley.
"Mounting of fragmentary metal scrolls."
Restaurator 2 (1975): 81-87.

940 Ogden, S. J. B.
"Conservation of library materials at the Newberry."
Guild of Book Workers Journal 14 (Fall 1975): 11-14.
(*See* A 5.2)

941 "Old negatives."
Kodak Industrial Camera 4 (1970): 11.

942 "Only top publishing management can change costly production practices, book binders agree."
Publishers' Weekly 207 (April 7, 1975): 40-43.

943 Organ, R. M.
Design for Scientific Conservation of Antiquities.
Washington, D. C.: Smithsonian Institution Press, 1968.
(*See* E 3.9)

944 Organ, R. M.
"Problems involved in controlling the museum climate for a temporary exhibition of ancient Japanese art."
In College Art Association, *Abstracts of Papers Delivered in Art History at Annual Meetings, 1969, 1970* (New York: College Art Association, 1972).

945 Orraca, J.
"The conservation of Photographic materials."
Bulletin of the American Institute for Conservation of Historic and Artistic Works 13, 2 (1973): 32-38.

946 O'Shea, C.
"Use of dewatering fluids in the conservation of waterlogged wood and leather."
Museums Journal 71, 2 (September 1971): 71-72.

947   Ostroff, E.
      Conserving and Restoring Photographic Collections.
      Washington, D. C.: American Association of Museums,
      1976.
      First published in *Museum News* 52, 8 (May 1974):
      42-45; 53, 1 (September 1974): 40-42, 48; 53, 3
      (November 1974): 42-45; and 53, 4 (December 1974):
      34-36.
      (*See* D 6.4)

948   Ostroff, E.
      "Photographic preservation: modern techniques."
      Paper presented at the Royal Photographic Society
      Symposium on the Recognition of Early Photographic
      Processes, their Care and Conservation, March 16, 1974.

949   Ostroff, E.
      "Preservation of photographs."
      Photographic Journal 107, 10 (1967): 309-14.
      Reprinted in Special Libraries Association, Picture
      Division *Picturescope* 18 (Summer 1970): 76-84.

950   Ostroff, E.
      "Restoration of Photographs by neutron activitation."
      Science 154 (October 7, 1966): 119-23.

951   Ostroff, E., and T. H. James.
      "Gelatine silver halide emulsion: a history."
      Journal of Photographic Science 20, 4 (1972): 146-48.

952   "Over a million waterlogged books and manuscripts."
      Unesco Courier 20 (January 1967): 30-33.

                              P

953   Pacey, P.
      Art Library Manual: A Guide to Resources and Practice.
      New York: Bowker, 1977.

954   Padfield, T.
       "The control of relative humidity and air pollution in
       show-cases and picture frames."
       Studies in Conservation 11 (1966): 8-30.
       (*See* B 5.6)

955   Padfield, T.
       "The design of museum show-cases."
       In Thomson, G., ed., *Contributions to the London
       Conference on Museum Climatology, 18-23 September
       1967* (London: International Institute for Conservation
       of Historic and Artistic Works, 1968), pp. 119-26.

956   Pakala, J. C.
       "The conservation of library materials."
       Library Scene 7, 1 (March 1978): 2-5.

957   Pallier, D.
       "La Bibliothèque nationale et les bibliothèques conserv-
       ant des fonds anciens" ("The National Library and
       libraries that preserve ancient collections").
       *Association des Bibliothécaires Français Bulletin
       d'Informations* 88 (1975): 140-41.

958   "Paper executive examines future needs, options."
       Publishers' Weekly 206 (October 7, 1974): 31.

959   "Paper orders increase but most observers foresee no
       immediate tightness in supplies."
       Publishers' Weekly 208 (August 4, 1975): 48.

960   "Paper problems, from press to bindery; a panel discus-
       sion."
       Publishers' Weekly 194 (September 2, 1968): 75-76.

961   "Paper spots microfilm."
       Reproduction Methods 10, 7 (1970): 40.

962   "Paper with a working life of five centuries."
       Publishers' Weekly 181 (April 1968): 40.

963 "Papermaking capacity will remain tight through 1980, study forecasts."
     Publishers' Weekly 206 (October 7, 1974): 31.

Parks, E. J.
     See 1344, Wilson, W. K.

964 Patton, F., and P. W. Darling.
     "The bee wing case: a preservation (tragedy) travesty."
     Library Journal 102 (April 1, 1977): 771-75.

965 Pear, C. B., ed.
     Magnetic Recording in Science and Industry.
     New York: Reinhold, 1967.
     (*See also* article from this work, cited separately, by P. R. Eldridge.)

966 Pearce, M. J.
     A Workbook of Analytical and Descriptive Bibliography.
     London: Clive Bingley, 1970.

967 Pearson, V.
     "Preparing art exhibits for travel."
     In Dudley, D. H., I. B. Wilkinson, and others, eds., *Museum Registration Methods* (Washington, D. C.: American Association of Museums, 1968), pp. 240-53.

968 Pedersen, H.
     "A method for fastening single leaves together for binding into volumes."
     Restaurator 2 (1975): 61-63.

Pelikan, A.
     See 640, King, A.

969 "Pennsylvania library flood damage $6.5 million."
     Wilson Library Bulletin 47 (September 1972): 5.

970 Perkinson, R.
     "The effects of light on museum objects."
     Museum News 53, 3 (1974): 5-7.

971 Perkinson, R., and R. Futernick.
"Questions concerning the design of paper pulp for repairing art on paper."
In Williams, J. C., ed., *Preservation of Paper and Textiles of Historical and Artistic Value* (Washington, D. C.: American Chemical Society, 1977), pp. 88-94.
(Advances in Chemistry Series, no. 164)

Perkinson, R.
See 350, Dolloff, F. W.

Perman, D. H.
See 633, Kent, G. O.

972 "Permanent and durable catalog cards."
Library Technology Reports, November 1975.
(Supplies and miscellaneous)

Petersen, D.
See 1270, Wächter, O.

973 Peterson, H. L.
Bibliography on the Preservation of Museum Specimens. Washington, D. C.: National Trust for Historic Preservation, 1972.

Petherbridge, G.
See 155, Blunn, D.

974 Petit, G.
"Conseils pour l'entretien des ouvrages anciens" ("Recommendations for the maintenance of ancient works").
Association des Bibliothécaires Français Bulletin d'Informations 85 (1974): 183.

975 Phelan, W. H., N. S. Baer, and N. Indictor.
"An evaluation of adhesives for use in paper conservation."
International Institute for Conservation of Historic and Artistic Works, Bulletin of the American Group 11, 2 (1971): 58-75.

Phelan, W. H.
See Baer, N. S.; 574, Indictor, N.

976 Philippot, P.
"Historic preservation: philosophy, criteria, guidelines."
In Timmons, S., ed., *Preservation and Conservation: Principles and Practices* (Washington, D. C.: National Trust for Historic Preservation in the U. S., Preservation Press, 1976), pp. 367-82.

977 Phillimore, E.
A Glossary of Terms Useful in Conservation.
Ottawa: Canadian Museums Association, 1976.

978 "Photocopying equipment."
Library Technology Reports, 1965- .
(*See* C 4.1)

979 Pickett, A. G., and M. M. Lemcoe.
Preservation and Storage of Sound Recordings.
Washington, D. C.: Library of Congress, 1959.

980 Pidek, J.
"Methods of reinforcing maps."
In Association of Canadian Map Libraries, *Proceedings of the Third Annual Conference, June 4-6, 1969* (Ottawa, Ontario: Association of Canadian Map Libraries, 1970), pp. 14-17.

981 Pieper, E.
Handbuch der praktischen Buchpflege ("Handbook of practical book care").
Munich: Moos, 1968.

982 Plenderleith, H. J.
"Preservation and restoration of documentary material—including any special problems of concern to the Pacific."
In *Source Materials Related to Research in the Pacific Area* (Canberra: Australian Government Publishing Service, 1973), pp. 50-59.

983 Plenderleith, H. J.
Preservation of Documentary Material in the Pacific Area: A Practical Guide.
Canberra: Australian Government Publishing Service for the Australian National Advisory Committee for Unesco, 1972.

984 Plenderleith, H. J.
The Preservation of Leather Bookbindings.
London: The Trustees of the British Museum, 1970.
Reprint of 1946 edition.

985 Plenderleith, H. J., and A. E. A. Werner.
The Conservation of Antiquities and Works of Art: Treatment, Repair and Restoration.
London: Oxford University Press, 1971.
2d ed.
(*See* E 3.8)

986 Pollard, G.
"On the repair of medieval bindings."
The Paper Conservator 1 (1976): 35-36.
(*See* D 3.3)

Pollock, V.
See 1298, Weiner, J.

987 Poole, C. H.
"Sistema de microficha en los Archivos Públicos del Canadá" ("Microfiche system in the public archives of Canada").
Boletín de la Asociación Archivística Argentina 4, 10 (January-April 1974): 32-33.

988 Poole, F. G.
"Current lamination policies of the Library of Congress."
American Archivist 39 (April 1976): 157-59.
(*See* D 1.3)

989   Poole, F. G.
          "Fumigate the area."
          American Libraries 9, 2 (February 1978): 74.
          (letter)

990   Poole, F. G.
          "Meeting summaries."
          College and Research Libraries News 39, 1 (January
          1978): 15, 18.
          (Summary of paper given by F. G. Poole at the annual
          meeting of the Music Library Association, August 16,
          1977)

991   Poole, F. G.
          "The physical protection of brittle and deteriorating
          documents."
          Library Scene 5 (June 1976): 9-11.
          (*See* D 1.2)

992   Poole, F. G.
          "Preservation."
          In Clark, R. L., ed., *Archive-Library Relations* (New
          York: Bowker, 1976), pp. 141-54.
          (*See* E 5.5)

993   Poole, F. G.
          "Preservation costs and standards."
          Special Libraries 59 (October 1968): 614-19.

994   Poole, F. G.
          "Report on pilot preservation project."
          Library of Congress Information Bulletin 28 (March 6,
          1969): 140-41.

995   Poole, F. G.
          "Report on the thirty-fourth annual conference of the
          Graduate Library School of the University of Chicago;
          deterioration and preservation of library materials."
          Library of Congress Information Bulletin 28 (August 21, 1969): A75-80.

996   Poole, F. G.
       "The research library and book conservation."
       Bollettino dell'Istituto di Patologia del Libro 29 (January-December 1970): 99-122.
       (*See* A 1.7)

997   Poole, F. G.
       "Some aspects of the conservation problem in archives."
       American Archivist 40 (April 1977): 163-71.
       (Paper presented at the SAA/NEH Conference on Priorities for Funding, January 1977, Chicago)
       (*See* E 5.4)

998   Poole, F. G.
       "Thoughts on the conservation of library materials."
       In Cunha, G. M., and N. P. Tucker, eds., *Library and Archives Conservation: The Boston Athenaeum's 1971 Seminar on the Application of Chemical and Physical Methods to be Conservation of Library and Archival Materials: May 17-21, 1971* (Boston: The Library of the Boston Athenaeum, 1972), pp. 13-25.

999   Poole, F. G.
       "William James Barrow."
       In Kent, A., and H. Lancour, eds., *Encyclopedia of Library and Information Science*, vol. 2 (New York: Marcel Dekker, 1969), pp. 257-70.

       Poole, F. G.
       See 315, Cunha, G. M.

1000   Poschmann, B., ed.
       Massenrestaurierung; Protokoll einer Arbeitstagung im Staatsarchiv Buckeburg, 1970 ("Mass restoration; report of a working conference in the Buckeburg State Archives, 1970").
       Gottingen: Vandenhoeck und Ruprecht, 1971.

1001   Potter, R. H.
       "New England Document Conservation Center; Proposal, November, 1970; Introduction, Prospectus, Draft Agreement."

In Cunha, G. M., and N. P. Tucker, eds., *Library and Archives Conservation: The Boston Athenaeum's 1971 Seminar on the Application of Chemical and Physical Methods to the Conservation of Library and Archival Materials: May 17-21, 1971* (Boston: The Library of the Boston Athenaeum, 1972), pp. 183-96.

1002   Poulos, A.
"Audio and video cassettes: friend or foe of the librarian?"
Special Libraries 63 (May-June 1972): 222-26.

1003   Powell, R.
"Case history of repair and rebinding of an eighth century vellum manuscript."
In Smith, P., *New Directions in Bookbinding* (New York: Van Nostrand Reinhold, 1974), pp. 174-83. (*See* D 3.4)

1004   Powell, R., and P. Waters.
"A technical description of the binding."
In Brown, T. J., ed., *The Stonyhurst Gospel of St. John* (Oxford: University Press, 1969).

1005   Powers, T.
"Bound to die."
New York Times Book Review, June 2, 1974, p. 55.

1006   "Practical problems."
Paper Conservation News (H. Wayne Eley Assoc., Inc.) 1, 3 (September 1973).
Entire issue.

1007   Prasad, B.
Problems of Misplacement, Mutilation and Theft of Books in Libraries.
Delhi: Motilal Barnarsidass, 1968.

1008   Preiss, D.
"Preserving pulp paper."
American Artist 39 (August 1975): 24.

1009   "Preservation office of LC."
        Library of Congress Information Bulletin 26 (November 2, 1967): 721-22.

1010   "Preservation research program of the Library of Congress."
        Library of Congress Information Bulletin 31 (September 15, 1972): A165-68.
        (*See* A 5.3)

1011   "Preservation supplement."
        Library of Congress Information Bulletin 31 (March 3, April 14, 1972): appendix.

1012   "Prism camera."
        Journal of the Society of Archivists 4 (October 1970): 145.

1013   "Procédé d'extinction des incendies; experimente aux Archives Nationales" ("Process of extinguishing fire; experiments at the National Archives").
        Gazette des Archives 94 (1976): 185-88.
        (Notes techniques)

1014   "Process to preserve rare books and manuscripts."
        Information; News/Sources/Profiles 6 (February 1974): 39-40.

1015   "Proper cleaning, handling, storing protects your investment in magnetic tape."
        Administrative Management 29 (December 1968): 34.

1016   "Protect your records while using them."
        Administrative Management 28 (July 1967): 28-29.

1017   Proudfoot, W. B.
        The Origin of Stencil Duplicating.
        London: Hutchinson, 1972.

1018   Public Archives of Canada.
        A Guide to the Preservation of Archival Materials.
        Quebec: Minister of Supplies and Services, 1977.
        (*See* B 2.2)

1019   Purafil, Inc.
           Purafil Odoroxidant: General Report.
           Chamblee, Georgia: Purafil, Inc., 1973.
           (Purafil technical bulletin, no. 101-C)

Q

1020   Quayle, E.
           "The art in binding."
           Wilson Library Bulletin 51 (January 1977): 408-418.

1021   Question of preservation: an anonymous gift of $100,000
           has made possible the establishment of a conservation
           laboratory."
           New York Public Library Bulletin 74 (October 1970):
           491-92.

1022   Quétin, M.
           "A propos de la Prévention et de la protection contre
           l'incendie" ("Concerning prevention and protection
           against fire").
           Gazette des Archives 92 (1975): 33-47.

1023   Quétin, M.
           L'équipment photographique des Archives en France;
           résultats et enseignements d'une enquête" ("Photo-
           graphic equipment in the archives of France; results
           and lessons of an investigation").
           Gazette des Archives 83 (1973): 229-41.

R

1024   Rachow, L. A.
           "Care and preservation of theatre library materials."
           Special Libraries 63 (January 1972): 25-30.

1025   Raffel, J. A., and R. Shishko.
       "Comparison of weeding criteria: a suboptimization."
       In *Systematic Analysis of University Libraries: An
       Application of Cost-Benefit Analysis to the M.I.T.
       Libraries*   (Cambridge: M.I.T.,   1969), pp. 15-19.

1026   Ramsey, R. W.
       "The New Brunswick flood relief program of 1973."
       Canadian Archivist 2, 4 (1973): 38-41.

1027   Rapa, M. S.
       "Mutilation of books: a case study of Kirori Mal College
       Library."
       Library Herald 11 (October 1969): 154-67.

1028   "Rare book division protected by new fire prevention
       system."
       Library of Congress Information Bulletin 34 (May 9,
       1975): 181.

1029   Ratcliffe, F. W.
       "Manchester University Library bindery: a study of
       library efficiency and management."
       Libri 20, 1-2 (1970): 77-88.

1030   Ratcliffe, F. W.
       "Margins in the manuscript and printed book."
       Penrose Annual 59 (1966): 217-34.

1031   Rath, F. L., and M. R. O'Connell, eds.
       *A Bibliography on Historical Organization Practices;
       Vol. 2: Care and Conservation of Collections.*
       Nashville: American Association for State and Local
       History, 1977.
       (*See* E 1.3)

1032   Rath, F. L., and M. R. O'Connell, eds.
       *Guide to Historic Preservation, Historical Agencies, and
       Museum Practices: A Selective Bibliography.*
       Cooperstown, New York: New York State Historical
       Association, 1970.

1033   Ray, C. T.
          "Flat electrode measurement of pH in printing paper."
          Tappi 55 (1972): 393-95.

1034   "Reading not dry."
          Liaison (Library Association Record), April 1968, p. 22.

1035   Ready, W. B.
          "Library books are different."
          Library Scene 3 (December 1974): 23-27.

1036   "Records storage; let the pro's do it."
          Purchasing 63, 8 (October 19, 1967): 75-78.

1037   Reddig, J. S.
          "Repairing history."
          American Libraries 5 (April 1974): 193-94.

1038   Reed, J. R.
          "Cost comparison of periodicals in hard copy and on
          microform."
          Microform Review 5 (July 1976): 185-92.

1039   Reed, J. R.
          Review of P. Dranov, *Microfilm: The Librarians' View,
          1976-77.*
          Journal of Micrographics 10 (January-February 1977):
          136.

1040   Reed, R.
          Ancient Skins, Parchments and Leathers.
          London and New York: Seminar Press, 1972.

       Reed, R.
          See 1290, Waters, P.

1041   Reichmann, F.
          "Bibliographic control of microforms."
          Microform Review 1 (October 1972): 279-80.

1042   "Relative humidity/temperature recorder."
          Library Journal 96 (August 1971): 2475.

1043 Rempel, S.
"A Conservation method for nitrate based photographic materials."
The Paper Conservator 2 (1977): 44-46.

1044 Rempel, S.
"The conservation of case photographs."
Archivaria 3 (Winter 1976-77): 103-108.
(Technical notes and information)

1045 Renaud, J.
"Le traitement et la conservation des documents" ("The treatment and conservation of documents").
Archives: Revue de l'Association des Archivistes du Quebec 1 (1975): 13-23.

1046 Rendell, K. W.
"The marking of books and manuscripts."
AB Bookman's Weekly 61 (January 30, 1978): 676-78.

1047 "Report of the joint consultation between the ICA and IFLA on the physical protection of books and documents. Paris, 19-21 November 1973."
Restaurator 2 (1975): 150-52.

1048 "Research Libraries Group developments."
Harvard Librarian 10, 3 (1974): 1-2.

1049 "Research libraries of the New York Public Library have announced the establishment of a conservation conservation laboratory."
Library of Congress Information Bulletin 29 (October 15, 1970): A141.

Resnik, M. A.
See 141, Berger, R.

1050 "Resolution to establish training standards and certification for conservators of art on paper."
Bulletin of the American Institute for Conservation of Historic and Artistic Works 14, 1 (1973): 98-116.

1051   "Restoration workshops."
       IFLA Journal 3, 2 (1977): 175.

1052   Rhoads, J. B.
       "Alienation and thievery: archival problems."
       American Archivist 29 (April 1966): 197-208.

       Rhoads, J. B.
       See 9, Adelstein, P. Z.

       Ribkin, T.
       See 322, Dadić, V.

1053   Rice, E. S.
       Fiche and Reel.
       Ann Arbor, Michigan: Xerox University Microfilms,
       1972.
       Rev. ed.

1054   Rice, J. W.
       "Requirements for bulk storage protection against
       insect damage."
       Textile Museum Journal 2, 4 (1969): 31-33.

1055   Richmond, M. L.
       "Attitudes of law librarians to theft and mutilation
       control methods."
       Law Library Journal   68 (February 1975): 60-70.
       (*See* B 4.5)

1056   Richtering, H.
       "Die Ersatzverfilmung des Schriftgutes der Registra-
       turen und die Archive" ("Replacement filming of
       written materials in records offices and archives").
       Der Archivar 24 (July 1971): cols. 245-56.
       Abstract in *American Archivist* 36 (January 1973): 99.

1057   Ries, J.
       "Die Anfaserungstechnik" ("Paper fiber technique").
       Nachrichten Vereinigung Schweizerischer Bibliothekare
       51, 2 (1975): 42-46.

1058 Ries, J.
"Der archiv-, buch- und graphikrestaurator in der Schweiz" ("Restorer of archives, books and graphics in Switzerland").
Nachrichten Vereinigung Schweizerischer Bibliothekare 44, 3 (1968): 65-67.

1059 Ries, J.
"Klebebänder" ("Adhesive tapes").
Nachrichten Vereinigung Schweizerischer Bibliothekare 45, 1 (1969): 4-7.

Riley, T. W.
See 1356, Yoho, C. H.

1060 Rineer, A. H.
"Conservation: the job that needs to be done."
In Doms, K., ed., "Preservation of library materials," *Pennsylvania Library Association Bulletin* 28 (November 1973), pp. 221-25.

1061 "Riunioni sulla conservazione dei libri e dei documenti (Grenoble, 28 agosto e Parigi, 19-21 novembre 1973)" ("Conference on conservation of books and documents [Grenoble, August 28, Paris, November 19-21, 1973] ").
Associazione Italiana Biblioteche Bollettino d'Informazioni 14 (January 1974): 61-62.

1062 Roberts, M.
"Guards, turnstiles, electronic devices, and the illusion of security."
College and Research Libraries 29, 4 (July 1968): 259-75.

1063 Roberts, M.
"Oversewing and the problem of book preservation in the research library."
College and Research Libraries 28 (January 1967): 17-24.
(*See* D 4.6)

1064   Roberts, M.
       "The role of the librarian in the binding process."
       Special Libraries 62 (October 1971): 413-20.
       (*See* D 4.4)

1065   Robinson, B.
       "Much more about laminated posters at the Princeton
       Public Library."
       Unabashed Librarian 6 (Winter 1973): 12-14.

1066   Robinson, L. S.
       "Micropublishing   subcommittee   and   the   Kalvar
       question."
       Microform Review 2 (October 1973): 255-56.
       Also published as "Tell it to the Times," *College and
       Research Libraries News* 11 (December 1973): 287-88.

1067   Rodgers, H. G., M. Idelson, R. F. W. Ciecuch, and S. M.
       Bloom.
       "The light stability of new Polaroid color prints."
       In Royal Photographic Society of Great Britain, *The
       Conservation of Colour Photographic Records* (London:
       Royal Photographic Society of Great Britain, 1974).

1068   Rodríguez Morales, L.
       "Algunas consideraciones sobre la restauración y re-
       habilitación de documentos."
       Boletin del Archivo General de la Nación 56, 211 (July-
       December 1966): 267-79.

1069   Rogers, J. W.
       "The rise of American edition binding."
       In Lehmann-Haupt, H., ed., *Bookbinding in America:
       Three Essays* (New York: R. R. Bowker, 1967), pp.
       129-156.

1070   Rogers, R. D., and D. C. Weber.
       "Binding and preservation."
       In *University Library Administration* (New York:
       Wilson, 1971), pp. 184-92.
       (*See* A 1.5)

1071   Roman, D.
        "Restoration of old faded photographs."
        Archives and Manuscripts   4 (August 1972): 7-10.

        Root, N. J.
        See 218, Burns, S.

1072   Rowlison, E. B.
        "Rules for handling works of art."
        Museum News 53, 7 (1975): 10-13.

1073   Royal Photographic Society of Great Britain.
        The Conservation of Colour Photographic Records.
        London: Royal Photographic Society of Great Britain,
        1974.
        (Monograph No. 1)
        Proceedings of a symposium, September 20, 1973.
        (*See also* articles from this work, cited separately, by
        D. Bermane, C. H. Giles, and H. G. Rodgers.)

1074   Royal Photographic Society of Great Britain.
        *The Recognition of Early Photographic Processes, Their
        Care and Conservation.*
        London: Royal Photographic Society of Great Britain,
        1974.
        Proceedings of a symposium, March 16, 1974.
        (*See also* articles from this work, cited separately, by
        C. Brian and M. F. Harker.)

1075   Rozkova, G. S.
        "Hygiene and restoration of book stock at libraries;
        some points of interest regarding the work of the Lenin
        State Library of the USSR."
        Restaurator 1 (1970): 191-97.
        (*See* A 5.4)

S

1076   Sadurska, I., and R. Kowalik.
        "Fungi preventive for for archival papers."
        Bollettino dell'Istituto di Patologia del Libro 27
        (January-June 1968): 37-47.

        Sadurska, I.
        See 650, Kowalik, R.

1077   Saffady, W.
        "Evaluating coin-operated copying equipment for
        library applications."
        Library Resources and Technical Services 20, (Spring
        1976): 115-22.
        (*See* C 4.2)

1078   Saffady, W.
        Micrographics.
        Littleton, Colorado: Libraries Unlimited, 1978.

1079   Saffady, W.
        "New developments in electrostatic copiers."
        American Archivist 38, 1 (January 1975): 67-75.
        (Technical notes)
        (*See* C 4.3)

1080   Saffady, W.
        "Teaching reprography."
        Journal of Education for Librarianship 15, 3 (Winter
        1975): 147-59.

1081   Sager, D. J.
        "Vandalism in libraries: how senseless is it?"
        Library Security Newsletter 1 (January 1975): 5.

1082   "St. Louis fire: panel reports findings."
        Society of American Archivists Newsletter, November
        1976, p. 4.

1083 Sajor, L. E.
"Preservation microfilming: why, what, when who, how."
Special Libraries 63 (April 1972): 195-201.
(*See* C 3.12)

1084 Salmon, S. R.
"User resistance to microforms in the research library."
Microform Review 3 (July 1974): 194-99.
(*See* C 3.9)

1085 "Salvaging miles of sodden books."
Life 61 (December 16, 1967): 34-35.

1086 "Sambindningskonferens i Solna Lugnar bokhandelsvänliga bibliotekarier" ("Conference in Solna on cooperative binding reassures librarians friendly to the book trade").
Biblioteksbladet 57, 1 (1972): 31-33.

1087 "San Francisco library saves smoke-damaged books."
Library Journal 97 (July 1972): 2331-32.

1088 Santen, V., and H. Crocker.
"Historical society records: guidelines for a protection program."
History News 27, 9 (September 1972): 193-200.
(AASLH technical leaflet 18)

Santucci, L.
See 1232, Triolo, L.

1089 Sargent, R.
Preserving the Moving Image.
Edited by G. Fleck. Washington, D. C.: Corporation for Public Broadcasting and the National Endowment for the Humanities, 1974.

1090 Sax, N. I., and others.
Dangerous Properties of Industrial Materials.
New York: Van Nostrand, Reinhold, 1975.

1091　Saxena, K. K.
　　　　"Preservation of manuscripts and documents."
　　　　Indian Librarian 22 (December 1967): 153-56.

1092　Schmelzer, M.
　　　　"Fire and water: book salvage in New York and in
　　　　Florence."
　　　　Special Libraries 59 (October 1968): 620-25.

1093　Schuller, A. J.
　　　　"Storing microforms."
　　　　Wisconsin Library Bulletin 68 (September 1972): 302.

1094　*"Sci-Tech News* news spotlights: freeze dried books."
　　　　Sci-Tech News 29 (January 1975): 27.

1095　Scilken, M. H.
　　　　"Children's books: binding costs and profits."
　　　　Unabashed Librarian 12 (Summer 1974): 26-27.

1096　Scilken, M. H.
　　　　"On binding practices."
　　　　Library Journal 99 (February 15, 1974): 513.
　　　　(letter)
　　　　Also published in *School Library Journal* 20 (February
　　　　1974): 3.

1097　"Scolar press prism for non-damaging copying of bound
　　　　volumes."
　　　　Library Technology Reports, May 1970.
　　　　(Photocopying equipment)

1098　Segal, J., and D. Cooper.
　　　　"The use of enzymes to release adhesives."
　　　　The Paper Conservator 2 (1977): 47-50.

1099　Sellers, D. Y., and R. Strassberg.
　　　　"Anatomy of a library emergency: how the Cornell
　　　　University Libraries dealt with flood damage and
　　　　developed plans to handle future emergencies."
　　　　Library Journal 98 (October 1, 1973): 2824-27.
　　　　(*See* B 3.8)

1100   Semĕnova, L. S.
       "25 let nauchno-proizvodstvennoi deiatel'nosti Iulia
       Petrovna Nuiksha" ("25th anniversary of the com-
       mencement of the scientific activity of Iulia Petrovna
       Nuiksha").
       Restaurator 1 (1970): 177-88.

1101   Serov, I.
       "Remont knizhnykh perepletov"   ("Repair of book
       bindings").
       Bibliotekar' no. 10 (1973): 59-61.

1102   Seymour, C. A.
       "Weeding the collection: a review of research on identi-
       fying obsolete stock; monographs."
       Libri 22, 2 (1972): 137-48.

1103   Shaffer, N. J.
       "Library of Congress pilot preservation project."
       College and Research Libraries 30 (January 1969):
       5-11.
       (*See* A 5.5)

1104   Shapiro, C., and L. Mason.
       "Preserving prints: basic conservation."
       In Fine Prints: Collecting, Buying, and Selling (New
       York: Harper and Row, 1976), pp. 77-95.

1105   Shapley, B.
       "The care and storage of magnetic tape."
       Data Processing Magazine 10 (April 1968): 80-81.
       (*See* D 6.11)

1106   Sharman, R. C.
       "New building for old: the transmigration of the
       Queensland State Archives."
       Archives and Manuscripts 3 (November 1968): 25-35.

1107   Shatzkin, L.
       "Publishing on permanent papers."
       Library Quarterly 40 (January 1970): 113-22.

1108   Shelley, K. L.
        "The future of conservation in research libraries."
        Journal of Academic Librarianship 1, 6 (January
        1976): 15-18.
        (*See* A 1.2)

        Shelley, M.
        See 68, Baer, N. S.

1109   Shepard, G. F.
        Review of A. J. Diaz, *Microforms in Libraries: A
        Reader.*
        Journal of Micrographics 10 (November-December
        1976): 100.

        Skishko, R.
        See 1025, Raffel, J. A.

        Shorland, Mrs. E. D.
        See 1348, Wood, R. D.

1110   "Shortages fading fast, at least temporarily."
        Publishers' Weekly 206 (December 2, 1974): 24-26.

1111   Shoulberg, R.
        "Stabilization using freeze-drying."
        In Morrison, R. C., G. M. Cunha, and N. P. Tucker, eds.,
        *Conservation Administration; Seminar on the Theoret-
        ical Aspects of the Conservation of Library and Archival
        Materials and the Establishment of Conservation Pro-
        grams, North Andover, Massachusetts, 1973* (North
        Andover, Massachusetts: New England Document
        Conservation Center and the Library of the Boston
        Athenaeum, 1975), pp. 151-68.

1112   Sillaste, G.
        "Restavratsiia i gigiena" ("Restoration and care").
        Bibliotekar' no. 11 (1975): 76-78.

        Simmel, E. C.
        See 555, Hoppe, R. A.

1113 Skiwska, J.
      "O konserwacji zbiorów w bibliotekach" ("Conserva-
      tion of library collections").
      Bibliotekarz 37, 7-8 (1970): 202-207.

1114 Sloan, W. J.
      "Projections: film rejuvenation and scratch removal."
      Film Library Quarterly 8, 3-4 (1975): 3-4.

1115 Slote, S. J.
      Weeding Library Collections.
      Littleton, Colorado: Libraries Unlimited, 1975.
      (Research Studies in Library Science, no. 14)

      Smith, J. C.
      See 1151, Spriestersbach, B.

1116 Smith, M. R.
      "Papyrus."
      Scholarly Publishing 6 (October 1974): 86-89.

1117 Smith, P.
      "Case history of *The Pilgrim's Progress* binding."
      In *New Directions in Bookbinding* (New York: Van
      Nostrand Reinhold Co., 1974), pp. 126-61.

1118 Smith, P.
      "Conservation versus creation?"
      In *New Directions in Bookbinding* (New York: Van
      Nostrand Reinhold Co., 1974), pp. 162-63.

1119 Smith, P.
      New Directions in Bookbinding.
      New York: Van Nostrand Reinhold, 1974.
      (*See also* articles from this work, cited separately, by
      A. Cains, R. Powell, and P. Smith.)

1120 Smith, P. B.
      "Preserving the word."
      The Changing Challenge—General Motors 4, 3 (1977):
      2-15.

1121   Smith, R. D.
       *A Comparison of Paper in Identical Copies of Books
       from the Lawrence University, the Newberry, and the
       New York Public Libraries.*
       Copenhagen: Restaurator Press, 1972.
       (Restaurator Supplement, no. 2)
       (*See* E 4.5)

1122   Smith, R. D.
       "The deacidification of paper and books."
       American Libraries 6 (February 1975): 108-10.
       (*See* D 5.7)

1123   Smith, R. D.
       "Design of a liquified gas mass deacidification system
       for paper and books."
       In Williams, J. C., ed., *Preservation of Paper and Textiles
       of Historical and Artistic Value* (Washington, D. C.:
       American Chemical Society, 1977), pp. 149-58.
       (Advances in Chemistry Series, no. 164)
       (*See* D 5.3)

1124   Smith, R. D.
       "The extension of book life."
       Library Binder 18, 2 (1970): 36-40.

1125   Smith, R. D.
       "Guidelines for preservation."
       Special Libraries 59 (May-June 1968): 346-52.
       (*See* A 1.6)

1126   Smith, R. D.
       "Maps: their deterioration and preservation."
       In Drazniowsky, R., ed., *Map Librarianship: Readings*
       (Metuchen, New Jersey: Scarecrow, 1975), pp. 395-410.
       Reprinted from *Special Libraries* 63 (February 1972):
       59-68.

1127   Smith, R. D.
       "New approaches to preservation."
       Library Quarterly 40 (January 1970): 139-71.

1128   Smith, R. D.
       "The nonaqueous deacidification of paper and books."
       Ph.D. dissertation, University of Chicago, 1970.

1129   Smith, R. D.
       "Paper deacidification: a preliminary report."
       Library Quarterly 36 (October 1966): 273-92.
       (*See* D 5.8)

1130   Smith, R. D.
       "Paper deacidification, part 3."
       Art Dealer and Framer, November 1976, pp. 40-46.
       (*See* D 5.4)

1131   Smith, R. D.
       "Paper deacidification, part 4."
       Art Dealer and Framer, December 1976, pp. 7-12.
       (*See* D 5.4)

1132   Smith, R. D.
       "Paper impermanence as a consequence of pH and
       storage conditions."
       Library Quarterly 39 (April 1969): 153-95.
       (*See* B 1.3)

1133   Smith, R. D.
       "The relative hazards of vapors from solvents used by
       conservators."
       Guild of Bookworkers Journal, Separate from   11, 2
       (1972-73).

1134   Smith, R. D.
       "Restoration of records."
       Records Management Quarterly 5 (1971): 27.

       Smith, R. D.
       See 1346, Winger, H. W.

1135   Smithsonian Institutiton. Office of Museum Programs.
       *Conservation Information for Museums; Audiovisual
       Loan Program, 1977-1978.*
       Washington, D. C.: Smithsonian Institution, 1977.

1136   "Smithsonian offers video tape and slide series on conservation."
        Society of American Archivists Newsletter, May 1976, p. 9.

1137   "Smyth cleat process."
        Library Technology Reports, May 1972.
        (Binding)

1138   Snell, Foster D., Inc.
        "Microfilm rejuvenation: an evaluation of three treatment services."
        Library Technology Reports, September 1973.
        (Microforms and equipment)

1139   Snyder, D. L.
        "Lamination as practiced in the California State Archives."
        Western Association of Map Libraries Information Bulletin 1, 3 (June 1970): 8-12.

1140   Snyder, D. L., and others.
        "Bibliography: map preservation."
        Western Association of Map Libraries Information Bulletin 1, 3 (June 1970): 23-25.

1141   Society of American Archivists. Archival Security Program.
        "A model law relating to library theft."
        Archival Security Newsletter (March 1977): 1, 8.

1142   "Society of American Archivists Council statement on energy conservation."
        Society of American Archivists Newsletter, May 1977, p. 2.

1143   Soderland, K. W.
        "Binding practice as related to the preservation of books: discussion."
        Library Quarterly 40 (January 1970): 137-38.

        Soha, J. M.
        See 1152, Spuck, W. H.

1144 Solvason, K. R.
"Air conditioning systems."
Canadian Building Digest no. 108 (December 1968).

1145 Sonnichsen, C. L.
"Dracula in the stacks."
Wilson Library Bulletin 51 (January 1977): 419-23.

1146 Souter, G. H.
"Delinquent readers: a study of the problems in university libraries."
Journal of Academic Librarianship 8, 2 (April 1976): 96-110.
(*See* B 4.4)

1147 Spawn, W.
"After the water comes."
In Doms, K., ed., "Preservation of library materials,"
Pennsylvania Library Association Bulletin 28 (November 1973), pp. 243-51.

1148 Spawn, W.
"Physical care of books and manuscripts."
In Peters, J., ed., *Book Collecting: a Modern Guide*
(New York: Bowker, 1977), pp. 136-58.
(*See* E 5.2)

Spawn, W.
See 1293, Waters, P.

1149 Spreitzer, F. F.
"Developments in copying, micrographics, and graphic communications, 1971."
Library Resources and Technical Services 16 (Spring 1972): 135-54.

1150 Spreitzer, F. F.
"Microfilm cartridges and cassettes."
Library Technology Reports, May 1972.
(Microforms and equipment)

1151   Spriestersbach, B., and J. C. Smith.
          "It should never happen to you!"
          Oklahoma Librarian 27 (January 1977): 8-11.

       Sproull, R. C.
          See 358, Dupuis, R. N.

1152   Spuck, W. H., R. J. Blackwell, and J. M. Soha.
          "Document restoration by digital image processing."
          American Archivist 39 (April 1976): 131-55.

1153   Stambolov, T.
          *Manufacture, Deterioration and Preservation of Leather:
          A Literature Survey of Theoretical Aspects and Ancient
          Techniques.*
          Amsterdam: Central Research Laboratory for Objects of
          Art and Science, 1969.
          (Paper presented at the plenary meeting of the ICOM
          Committee for Conservation)

1154   "Stamping: a survey of the state of the art."
          Society of American Archivists Newsletter, November
          1975, p. 5.

1155   "Standards for reprint publishing; recommendations for
          control of editorial quality."
          Special Libraries 63 (July 1972): 359.
          (Report of the Rare Book Libraries' Conference on
          Facsimiles)
          (*See* C 3.10)

1156   Stanojlovic, L.
          "Evolution de la restauration."
          *Archives: Revue de l'Association des Archivistes du
          Québec* 1 (1975): 4-12.

1157   Stanojlovic, L.
          "Restauration des livres et du matériel d'archives"
          ("Restoration of books and archival materials").
          *Archives: Revue de l'Association des Archivistes du
          Québec* 2 (1975): 135-38.

1158   "State library to assist in preservation of paper."
       Bookmark 31 (July 1972): 177.

1159   "Statut du corps des restaurateurs spécialistes; décret du
       27 mars 1973" ("Statute of the body of restoration
       specialists; executive order of March 27, 1973").
       Bulletin des Bibliothèques de France 18 (July 1973):
       349-52.

1160   Stender, W. W., and E. Walker.
       "The National Personnel Records Center fire: a study
       in disaster."
       American Archivist 37 (October 1974): 521-49.
       (*See* B 3.7)

1161   Stephenson, G. A.
       "Some notes on the care of prints and photographs at
       the National Portrait Gallery."
       Special Libraries Association, Picture Division *Picture-scope* 20 (Winter 1972): 174-79.

1162   Sterman, C. A.
       "New microfilm processing and storage standards."
       Records Management Journal 10, 2 (Summer 1972):
       20-23.

1163   Stevenson, A.
       "Paper as bibliographical evidence."
       In Jones, J. B., ed., *Readings in Descriptive Bibliography*
       (Kent, Ohio: Kent State University Press, 1974),
       pp. 128-47.

1164   Stevenson, A.
       "The Problem of the Missale Speciale.
       London: The Bibliographical Society, 1967.

1165   Steward, S.
       "Hunting and caring for books"
       In *Book Collecting: A Beginners Guide.*
       (New York: E. P. Dutton, 1973), pp. 236-54.

1166   Stipe, R. E.
       "Comments on 21 leading conservation-preservation organizations."
       In Timmons, S., ed., *Preservation and Conservation: Principles and Practices* (Washington, D. C.: National Trust for Historic Preservation in the U. S., Preservation Press, 1976), pp. 71-85.

1167   Stolow, N.
       "The action of environment on museum objects. Part I: humidity, temperature, atmospheric pollution."
       Curator 9, 3 (September 1966): 175-85.
       (*See* B 1.4)

1168   Stolow, N.
       "The action of environment on museum objects. Part II: light."
       Curator 9, 4 (December 1966): 298-306.
       (*See* B 1.5)

1169   Stolow, N.
       "Conservation policy and the exhibition of museum collections."
       Journal of the American Institute for Conservation 16, 2 (February 1977): 12-20.
       (Paper presented at the 4th annual meeting of the American Institute for Conservation of Historic and Artistic Works, May 29-June 1, 1976)
       (*See* B 5.2)

1170   Stolow, N.
       Controlled Environment for Works of Art in Transit. London: Butterworths, 1966.

1171   Stolow, N.
       "Environmental security."
       In Keck, C. K., and others, *A Primer on Museum Security* (Cooperstown, New York: New York State Historical Association, 1966), pp. 39-49.

1172   Stolow, N.
       "The ideal container for the travel of works of art."
       In Dudley, D. H., I. B. Wilkinson, and others, eds.,

Museum Registration Methods   (Washington, D. C.: American Association of Museums, 1968), pp. 254-59.

1173   Stolow, N.
"Fundamental case design for humidity-sensitive museum collections."
Museum News Technical Supplement, no. 11, 1966.

1174   Stolow, N.
"Light and its effects on museum objects."
In Keck, C. K., and others, *A Primer on Museum Security*   (Cooperstown, New York: New York State Historical Association, 1966), pp. 51-58.

1175   Stolow, N.
"Standards for the care of works of art in transit."
In Thomson, G., ed., *Contributions to the London Conference on Museum Climatology, 18-23 September 1967* (London: International Institute for Conservation of Historic and Artistic Works, 1968), pp. 271-84.

1176   Stoner, J. H.
Review of S. Timmons, ed., *Preservation and Conservation: Principles and Practices*.
Journal of the American Institute for Conservation 17, 1 (Fall 1977): 70-71.

1177   Strassberg, R.
"Books: fire and water damage: a selective bibliography on preventative measures and restoration techniques."
Cornell University Libraries Bulletin 181 (January 1973): 31-33.

1178   Strassberg, R.
Disaster Prevention and Control: A Select Bibliography.
Ithaca, New York: Cornell University Libraries, 1977.
(*See* E 1.2)

1179   Strassberg, R., comp.
Manual of Manuscript Processing Procedures.
Ithaca, New York: Cornell University Libraries, 1973.

1180   Strassberg, R.
            "The use of fumigants in archival repositories."
            American Archivist 41 (January 1978): 25-36.

        Strassberg, R.
            See 1099, Sellers, D. Y.

        Strom, S. C.
            See 378, Edelglass, E. T.

1181   Stuhrke, R. A.
            "The development of permanent paper."
            In Williams, J. C., ed., *Preservation of Paper and Textiles
            of Historical and Artistic Value* (Washington, D. C.:
            American Chemical Society, 1977), pp. 24-36.
            (Advances in Chemistry Series, no. 164)
            (*See* E 4.1)

1182   Sugar, C. L. de.
            "Travaux de remise en état de la Bibliothèque Nationale
            de Florence" ("Work of restoration at the National
            Library of Florence").
            *Association des Bibliothécaires Français Bulletin d'
            Informations* 58 (1968): 9-13.

1183   Suelflow, A. R.
            "Archives: their care, preservation and maintenance."
            Catholic Library World 46 (September 1974): 62-67.

        Sullivan, R. C.
            See 669, LaHood, C. G.

1184   Surrency, E. C.
            "Freeze-dried books."
            Library Journal 99 (September 15, 1974): 2108-2109.
            (letter)

1185   Swayne, L. H.
            "Fire protection at the National Archives Building."
            Fire Journal 69, 1 (January 1975): 65-67.

1186   Szajko, U.
"Na temat kursu konserwacji; refleksje" ("About topics of a course in conservation; reflections").
Bibliotekarz 40, 2 (1973): 52-53.

T

Tang, L. C.
See 632, Kelly, G. B.

1187   Tanselle, G. T.
"Bibliographers and the library."
Library Trends 25 (April 1977): 745-762.
(*See* D 4.1)

1188   Tanselle, G. T.
"The bibliographical description of paper."
Studies in Bibliography 24 (1971): 27-67.
Reprinted in Jones, J. B., ed., *Readings in Descriptive Bibliography* (Kent, Ohio: Kent State University Press, 1974), pp. 71-115.

1189   Tanselle, G. T.
"The bibliographical description of patterns."
Studies in Bibliography 23 (1970): 71-102.

1190   Tanselle, G. T.
"Book jackets, blurbs, and bibliographers."
Library (5th series) 26 (June 1971): 91-134.

1191   Tanselle, G. T.
"A system of color identification for bibliographical description."
Studies in Bibliography 20 (1967): 203-234.

TAPPI.
See Technical Association of the Pulp and Paper Industry.

1192   Tarkiainen, K.
         "Avsyrning och maskinlel laminering av arkivhandlingar;
         en litteraturstudie."
         Svenska Ark   17 (1975): 66-79.

1193   "Task of repairing the flood-damaged libraries of Florence."
         Book Collector   18 (Autumn 1969): 364-65.

1194   Tauber, M. F., ed.
         "Conservation of library materials."
         Library Trends   4 (January 1956): 215-334.
         (*See*   E 5.11)

1195   Tauber, M. F., ed.
         *Library   Binding Manual: A   Handbook   of   Useful
         Procedures for the Maintenance of Library   Volumes.*
         Boston: Library Binding Institute, 1972.
         (*See*   D 4.3)

1196   Tauber, M. F.
         "Progress in binding and conservation."
         Rub-Off   19 (September 1968):   1-4.

1197   Teague, S. J.
         "New York Times: Kalvar microfilm problem."
         MICRODOC   13, 2 (1974):   62.

1198   Technical   Association   of   the   Pulp   and   Paper   Industry.
         TAPPI Standards and Suggested Methods.
         New York: TAPPI, 1966- .
         (loose leaf)

1199   Technical   Association   of   the   Pulp   and   Paper   Industry.
         TAPPI Standards for Paper Permanence and Durability.
         Atlanta, Georgia: TAPPI, 1977.

1200   "Temple   University   books   restored   by   salvage   firm."
         Library   Journal   97 (November   15,   1972):   3667.

1201   "Temple University Library destroyed by fire."
         Library Journal   97 (September 15, 1972): 2796-97.

1202   "Test devices used in binding standards."
       Library Technology Reports, July 1967.
       (Binding)

1203   "The worse they get."
       Wilson Library Bulletin   51 (November 1976): 217.

1204   "There is a constant tension in any library between the wish
       to use its contents and the need to preserve them."
       Book Collector 22 (Autumn 1973): 367.

1205   Thomas, D., and J. Flink.
       "Rapid drying of water soaked books using a microwave
       tunnel dryer."
       Restaurator 2 (1975): 105-119.

1206   Thomas, G. W.
       "Hypo and archival quality."
       Microfilm Techniques 3, 5 (September 1974): 21, 26.

1207   Thomas, J. J.
       "Alkaline printing papers: promise and performance."
       Library Quarterly 40 (January 1970): 99-107.

1208   Thompson, E. A.
       "Restoration and preservation of books and docu-
       ments."
       Records Management Quarterly 5 (January 1971):
       13-16.

1209   Thompson, S. O.
       "Ownership marks on books: historical view."
       AB Bookman's Weekly 61 (January 30, 1978): 650-74.

1210   Thomson, G.
       "Annual exposure to light within museums."
       Studies in Conservation 12 (1967): 26-35.

1211   Thomson, G.
       Conservation and Museum Lighting.
       London: Museums Association, 1970.
       (Museums Association information sheet)

1212   Thomson, G., ed.
       Contributions to the London Conference on Museum Climatology, 18-23 September 1967.
       London: International Institute for Conservation of Historic and Artistic Works, 1968.
       rev. ed.
       (*See also* articles from this work, cited separately, by T. H. Garver, A. J. Haagen-Smit, J. B. Harris, F. H. Howorth, T. Padfield, and N. Stolow.)

1213   Thomson, G.
       "Controlled environment at the National Gallery, London."
       International Institute for Conservation of Historic and Artistic Works Newsletter 4, 3 (1967): 9.

1214   Thomson, G., and E. T. Hall.
       "An ultraviolet monitor for museums."
       Archaeometry 10 (1967): 120-126.

1215   3M Company. Magnetic Audio/Video Products Division.
       "Handling and storage of Magnetic recording tape."
       (Technical publication)

1216   3M Company. Magnetic Products Division.
       "The handling and storage of video recording tape."
       Video Talk 1, 2 (1968): 1-6.

1217   Time-Life Books.
       Caring for Photographs: Display, Storage, Restoration.
       New York: Time Inc., 1972.

1218   Timmons, S., ed.
       Preservation and Conservation: Principles and Practices.
       Washington, D. C.: National Trust for Historic Preservation in the U. S., Preservation Press, 1976.
       (Proceedings of the North American International Regional Conference, Williamsburg, Va. and Philadelphia, September 10-16, 1972)
       (*See also* articles from this work, cited separately, by R. D. Buck, J. M. Fitch, C. K. Keck, L. J. Majewski, P. E. Michaels, P. Philippot, and R. E. Stipe.)
       (*See* E 3.4)

Timmons, S.
See 1176, Stoner, J. H.

1219 Tombor, T.
"Edificio e preservazione; considerazioni sulla con-
cezione dell'edificio di una biblioteca di conservazione"
("Building and preservation; considerations in building a
library to insure book preservation").
Bollettino dell'Istituto di Patologia del Libro 30 (Jan-
uary-June 1971): 101-112.
(*See* B 2.6)

1220 Torrance, J. S.
"A justification of air-conditioning in libraries."
Journal of Librarianship 7, 3 (July 1975): 199-206.
(*See* B 2.3)

1221 Totten, H. L.
"Selection of library materials for storage: a state of the
art."
Library Trends 19 (January 1971): 341-351.

1222 "Tougher security measures adopted by libraries."
Library Journal 101 (March 15, 1976): 764.

1223 "Training programs in the conservation of artistic works."
*Bulletin of the American Institute for Conservation of
Historic Works* 15, 1 (1974): 28-38.

Tapani, R. di
See 1232, Triolo, L.

1224 "Treatment of cloth-bound books; pamphlets (paperbacks);
manuscripts and letters; newspaper clippings."
Rub-Off 18 (September 1967): 9-10.

1225 Trelles, O. M.
"Protection of libraries."
Law Library Journal 66 (August 1973): 241-58.
Also published in Katz, W. A., and S. Gaherty, eds.,
Library Literature 4—The Best of 1973 (Metuchen,
New Jersey: Scarecrow, 1974), pp. 177-212.

1226   "Trento: raccolte librarie" ("Trento: library collections").
       Accademie e Biblioteche d'Italia   40 (July-October
       1972): 353-56.

1227   Tribolet, H. W.
       "Binding practice as related to the preservation of
       books."
       Library Quarterly 40 (January 1970): 128-37.
       (*See* D 3.8)

1228   Tribolet, H. W.
       "The preservation of manuscripts."
       Manuscripts 18, 4 (Fall 1966): 6-10.

1229   Tribolet, H. W.
       "Rare book and paper repair techniques."
       History News 25, 3 (March 1970): 53-64.
       (AASLH technical leaflet 13)
       (*See* D 1.8)

1230   Tribolet, H. W.
       "Restoration in Florence."
       Manuscripts 20, 4 (Fall 1968): 20-36.
       (*See* B 3.10)

1231   Tribolet, H. W.
       "Trends in preservation."
       Library Trends 13 (1964-65): 208-14.
       (*See* E 5.10)

1232   Triolo, L., R. di Trapani, and L. Santucci.
       "Resistenza e stabilità della carta. VII: Trattamento
       con composti fungicidi" ("Resistance and stability of
       paper VII: Treatment with fungicides").
       Bollettino dell'Istituto di Patologia del Libro 27 (June-
       December 1968): 207-224.

1233   Trobas, K.
       "Anfaserung—Anfaserungsgeräte—Faserstoffe" ("Paper
       fiber—paper fiber equipment—fiber pulp").
       Der Archivar 25 (November 1972): cols. 401-408.

1234 Trobas, K.
"Möglichkeiten und Nebenwirkungen bei der Anfaserung unter besonderer Berucksichtigung der pH-Wertänderung" ("Contingencies and secondary effects in paper fiber under special consideration for change of pH values").
Der Archivar 27 (February 1974): cols. 65-70.

1235 Tröger, R., and G. Müller.
"Langzeitkonservierung biologisch geschädigter Bibliotheksbestände" ("Long-time conservation of biologically damaged library materials").
Zentralblatt für Bibliothekswesen 88 (June 1974): 357-61.

1236 Tröger, R., and others.
"Untersuchungen zur anwendung und wirkungsweise von mikrobenvernichtenden substanzen bei der papierrestaurierung und -Konservierung" ("Analyses of the application and working of substances esterminating microbes in the restoration and preservation of books").
Zentralblatt für Bibliothekswesen 83 (June-July 1969): 342-372.

1237 Tryon, R. H.
Flood and Fire Damage in Archives: A Select Bibliography.
Madison, Wisconsin: State Historical Society of Wisconsin, 1977.

Tucker, N. P.
See 316, Cunha, G. M.; 662, Kusterer, J. E.; 812, Morrison, R. C.; 1354, Wrotenbery, C. R.

Turner, S. J.
See 378, Edelglass, E. T.

1238 Tydeman, P. A.
"A simple method for contact beta-radiography of paper."
Paper Maker 153, 6 (1967): 42-48, 65.

1239   Tyrrell, A.
        Basics of Reprography.
        London and New York: Focal Press, 1972.

                                    U

1240   "Underground vaults and commercial records storage
        centers."
        Office 78 (September 1973): 82-87.

1241   Unesco.
        *Conservation of Cultural Property with Special Refer-
        ence to Tropical Conditions.*
        Paris: Unesco, 1968.
        (Unesco's Museums and Monuments, no. 11)
        Prepared in cooperation with the International Center
        for the Study of the Preservation and Restoration of
        Cultural Property, Rome.

1242   United Kingdom. National Reprographic Centre for Docu-
        mentation.
        "A proposal to investigate methods of determining the
        storage life of Diazo and Vesicular microfilms."
        Microfilm Review 4 (April 1975): 92-95.

        United States. Department of Agriculture.
        See 340, Department of Agriculture.

        United States. Library of Congress.
        See Library of Congress.

        United States. National Archives and Records Service.
        See National Archives and Records Service.

1243   University of California. Task Group on Preservation of
        Library Materials.
        "Report."
        Unpublished internal document, 1978.

1244   University of Wisconsin-Madison Library System. Preserva-
         tion of Library Materials Committee.
         Statement on the Conservation of Library Materials.
         Madison: University of Wisconsin-Madison Library
         System, 1976.
         (*See* A 2.3)

                                    V

1245   Vaccaro Sofia, E.
         "La Biblioteca di stato di Monaco e il suo Istituto di
         restauro" ("Monaco state library and its Institute for
         restoration").
         Bollettino dell'Istituto di Patologia del Libro 25 (July-
         December 1966): 213-240.

1246   Vaccaro Sofia, E.
         "Restoration laboratory of the Alfonso Gallo Institute
         of Book Pathology."
         Unesco Bulletin for Libraries 20 (March-April 1966):
         78-82.

1247   Vaccaro Sofia, E.
         "Vita e attivita' istituzionale dell'Istituto di patologia
         del libro Alfonso Gallo" ("Institutional life and activity
         of the Alfonso Gallo institute of book pathology").
         Accademie e Biblioteche d'Italia 35 (November 1967):
         462-67.

1248   Vaillant, P.
         "Conservation et communication des livres anciens dans
         les bibliothèques municipales" ("Conservation and
         communication of ancient books in the public
         libraries").
         *Association des Bibliothécaires Français Bulletin d'
         Informations* 84 (1974): 133-35.

1249   Vaisey, D. G.
       "The new manuscripts repair room."
       Bodleian Library Record 9, 1 (1973): 2-3.

       Vaisey, D. G.
       See 788, Michelmore, D.

1250   Valentín Rodrigo, N.
       "Contaminación microbiológica en museos, archivos y
       bibliotecas" ("Microbiological contamination in
       museums, archives, and libraries").
       Revista de Archivos, Bibliotecas y Museos 77 (July-
       December 1974): 747-761.

1251   "Valuable Danish documents salvaged by freeze-drying."
       Library Journal 97 (March 15, 1972): 961.

1252   Van Altena, W. F.
       "Envelopes for the archival storage of processed astro-
       nomical photographs."
       American Astronomical Society Photo Bulletin 1
       (1975): 18-19.

1253   Van Altena, W. F.
       "Report of the subgroup on the storage of astronomical
       plates for archival purposes."
       American Astronomical Society Photo Bulletin 2
       (1972): 15-17.

1254   Van Tassel, D.
       Computer Security Management.
       Englewood Cliffs, New Jersey: Prentice Hall, 1972.

1255   "Vandalism at Stanford: $15,000 damage claimed."
       Library Journal 96 (May 15, 1971): 1659-60.

1256   Vanderbilt, P.
       "Filing your photographs: some basic procedures."
       History News 21, 6 (June 1966): 117-24.
       (AASLH technical leaflet 36)

1257 Vandyke-Lee, D. J.
"Conservation of Tandu."
Studies in Conservation 21 (May 1976): 74-78.

Vatican Library.
See 144, Biblioteca Apostolica Vaticana.

1258 Veaner, A. B.
"Danger from trichloroethylene."
Microform Review 5 (April 1976): 89.

1259 Veaner, A. B.
The Evaluation of Micropublications: A Handbook for Librarians.
Chicago: American Library Association, 1971.
(Library Technology Program Publication No. 17)

1260 Veaner, A. B.
"Microreproduction and micropublication technical standards: what they mean to you, the user."
Microform Review 3 (April 1974): 80-84.
Revision of article with similar title in *Choice* 5 (September 1968): 7.
(*See* C 2.5)

1261 Veaner, A. B., and A. M. Meckler.
International Microforms in Print, 1974-75; A Guide to Microforms on Non-United States Micropublishers.
Weston, Connecticut: Microform Review, 1974.

1262 Veaner, A. B., and A. M. Meckler.
Microform Market Place, 1974-75; An International Directory of Micropublishers.
Weston, Connecticut: Microform Review, 1974.

1263 Venter, J. S. M.
The Aging and Preservation of Paper; A Development Study Submitted to the Pulp and Paper Research Steering Committee.
Pretoria: Council for Scientific and Industrial Research, 1966.

1264   Vickers, J.
         "Living with humidity; part 1."
         British Journal of Photography   123 (1976): 364-67.

1265   Vickers, J.
         "Living with humidity; part 2."
         British Journal of Photography   123 (1976): 392-96.

1266   Virden, K.
         "Hurricane damage to libraries in South Texas."
         Texas Library Journal 43 (1967): 164-65.

1267   "Virginia records salvaged."
         Society of American Archivists Newsletter, July 1977,
         p. 4.

1268   Vonlanthen, G.
         "Lederkonservierung: stiefkind vieler bibliotheken"
         ("Leather conservation: stepchild in many libraries").
         Nachrichten Vereinigung Schweizerischer Bibliothekare
         46, 2 (1970): 63-64.

1269   Vyskočil, J.
         "The central conservation workshop of the State
         Library of the Czechoslovak Socialist Republic."
         Unesco Bulletin for Libraries   20 (May-June 1966):
         126-28.

W

         W. J. Barrow Research Laboratory.
         See Barrow Research Laboratory.

1270   Wächter, O.
         "Das bleichen von alten papieren."
         In Petersen, D., *Das Alte Buch als Aufgabe für
         Naturwissenschaft und Forschung.*   (Wolfenbüttel,
         1977).

1271 Wächter, O.
"Die Konservierung von Holzschliffpapieren und Zeitungsbänden" ("Preservation of wood-pulp papers and newspaper volumes").
Biblos 23, 1 (1974): 22-36.

1272 Wächter, O.
Restaurierung und Erhaltung von Büchern, Archivalien, und Graphiken: mit Berücksichtigung des Kulturgüterschutzes laut Haager Konvention von 1954 ("Restoration and preservation of books, archival and graphic materials: with consideration of the safeguarding of cultural values in accordance with the Hague Convention of 1954").
Graz: H. Bohlaus, 1975.

1273 Wagner, R. W.
"Motion picture restoration."
American Archivist 32 (April 1969): 125-32.
(*See* D 6.10)

1274 Wagner, R. W.
"Preservation and restoration of photographic materials through nuclear and ultra-sonic methods."
Illinois Libraries 53 (January 1971): 10-17.

1275 Wakeman, G.
Victorian Book Illustration; The Technical Revolution.
Newton Abbott: David and Charles, 1973.

1276 Walch, T.
Archives and Manuscripts: Security.
Chicago: Society of American Archivists, 1977.
(Basic Manual Series)
(*See* B 4.1)

1277 Walker, B.
"Morpholine deacidification of whole books."
In Williams, J. C., ed., *Preservation of Paper and Textiles of Historical and Artistic Value* (Washington, D. C.: American Chemical Society, 1977), pp. 72-86.
(Advances in Chemistry Series, no. 164)

1278 Walker, B.
"Specifications for permanent/durable book papers."
American Archivist 38 (July 1975): 405-416.
(Technical notes)

Walker, E.
See 1160, Stender, W. W.

1279 Walker, G.
"Preservation efforts in larger U. S. academic libraries."
College and Research Libraries 36 (January 1975): 39-44.
(*See* A 1.3)

1280 Wall, J.
"The case for a central photographic archive in colour."
Journal of the Society of Archivists 3 (October 1969): 566-70.

1281 Wall, J.
"Colour separations and photographic archives."
Photographic Journal 110 (March 1970): 98-101.

1282 Wall, J.
"Overcoming the problems of permanency in colour archives."
Photographic Journal 107 (April 1967): 141-45.

1283 Walters, A. H., and E. H. Hueck-Van Der Plas, eds.,
Biodeterioration of Materials:
New York: Halsted Press Division, Wiley, 1972.
(Proceedings of the 2d International Biodeterioration Symposium, Lunteren, Netherlands, 1971)

1284 Walters, A. H., and J. J. Elphick, eds.
Biodeterioration of Mat*erials: Microbiological and Allied Aspects.*
Amsterdam: Elsevier Publishing Co., 1968.
(Proceedings of the 1st International Biodeterioration Symposium, Southampton, 9-14 September 1968)

Walton, C. C.
See 315, Cunha, G. M.

1285 Wardle, D. B.
Document Repair.
London: Society of Archivists, 1971.

1286 "Water alarm."
International Institute for Conservation of Historic and Artistic Works, Bulletin of the American Group 12, 1 (1971): 34.

1287 Waterer, J. W.
A Guide to the Conservation and Restoration of Objects Made Wholly or in Part of Leather.
London: G. Bell & Sons, 1972.

1288 Waters, P.
"Book restoration after the Florence floods."
Penrose Annual 62 (1969): 83-93.
(*See* B 3.9)

1289 Waters, P.
"Deacidification, lamination and the use of polyester film encapsulation."
Western Association of Map Libraries Information Bulletin 6, 3 (1975): 19-21.
Also published in *Special Libraries Association, Geography and Map Division Bulletin* 99 (March 1975): 46-48.

1290 Waters, P.
"Problems of restoring old books."
In Reed, R., ed., *Symposium on Printing* (Leeds: Leeds Philosophical and Literary Society, 1971), pp. 27-34.

1291 Waters, P.
Procedures for Salvage of Water-Damaged Library Materials.
Washington, D. C.: Library of Congress, 1975.
(Library of Congress Publications on Conservation of Library Materials)
(*See* B 3.6)

1292   Waters, P.
        "Requirements for an international center for preservation of books and manuscripts."
        Bollettino dell'Istituto di Patologia del Libro 29 (January-December 1970): 60-74.

1293   Waters, P., R. McComb, C. Horton, and W. Spawn.
        "Does freeze-drying save waterlogged books or doesn't it? Salvaging a few 'facts' from a flood of (alleged) misinformation."
        American Libraries   6 (July-August 1975): 422-23.

        Waters, P.
        See 542, Hey, M.; 1004, Powell, R.

1294   Watson, A. J.
        "Manufacturing and environmental factors affecting the permanence of paper."
        Archives and Manuscripts   6 (August 1976): 285-91.
        (*See* B 1.1)

1295   Watson, T. C.
        "Archive and costume storage."
        Curator 19, 1 (March 1976): 29-36.

1296   Watts, C. E.
        A Guide to the Better Care of LP and Stereo Records.
        Middlesex, England: Cecil E. Watts, Ltd., 1970.

        Weber, D. C.
        See 1070, Rogers, R. D.

1297   Weidner, M. K.
        "Damage and deterioration of art on paper due to ignorance and the use of faulty materials."
        Studies in Conservation 12 (1967): 5-25.

1298   Weiner, J., and V. Pollock.
        Permanence.
        Appleton, Wisconsin: Institute of Paper Chemistry, 1970.
        (Bibliographic series no. 213, supplement 1)

Weiner, J.
See 222, Byrne, J.

1299   Weinstein, R. A.
"If you collect photographs. . . ."
Hawaii Library Association Journal 29, 1 (June 1972):
15-17.

1300   Weinstein, R. A., and L. Booth.
Collection, Use and Care of Historical Photographs.
Nashville: American Association of State and Local
History, 1977.
(*See* D 6.1)

1301   Weiss, D. A.
"Book preservation shouldn't be a problem."
Library Scene 4 (March 1975): 16.

1302   Weiss, D. A.
"Editorial: library binding, circa 1974."
Library Scene 3 (September 1974): 11.

1303   Weiss, D. A.
"Library Binding Institute."
In Kent, A., and H. Lancour, eds., *Encyclopedia of
Library and Information Science*, vol. 2 (New York:
Marcell Dekker, 1969), pp. 510-12.

1304   Weiss, D. A.
"The Library Binding Institute: a mini profile."
Library Scene 7, 1 (March 1978): 11-12.

1305   Weiss, D. A.
"What is your collection worth? (And what are you
doing about it?)"
Library Scene 3 (June 1974): 9-10.

1306   Weiss, S. E.
"Proper exhibition lighting: protecting collections from
damage."
Technology and Conservation 1 (Spring 1977): 20-25.
(*See* B 5.3)

1307   Welch, C. E.
         "Protection from fire in libraries."
         New England Journal of Medicine 287 (1972): 881-82.

1308   Welch, W. L.
         "Preservation and restoration of authenticity in sound
         recordings."
         Library Trends 21 (July 1972): 83-100.
         (*See* D 6.6)

1309   Welch, W. L.
         "Recorded music and re-recording processes."
         American Archivist 31 (October 1968): 379-90.

1310   Wells, J. A.
         "Conservation of motion pictures, microfilms and
         photographs."
         In Library Association of Australia, *1969 Conference
         Proceedings, Adelaide*
         (Library Association of Australia, 1971), pp. 401-406.

1311   Wendelbo, Ø.
         "Freeing of papyri from cargonnage."
         Restaurator 2 (1975): 41-52.

1312   Wendelbo, Ø., and B. Fosse.
         "Protein 'surgery,' a restoring procedure applied on
         paper."
         Restaurator 1 (1970): 245-48.

1313   Werner, A. E.
         "Conservation and display: environmental control."
         Museums Journal 72 (September 1972): 58-60.
         (*See* B 5.5)

       Werner, A. E. A.
         See 985, Plenderleith, H. J.

1314   Wessel, C. J.
         "Deterioration of library materials."
         In Kent, A., and H. Lancour, eds., *Encyclopedia of
         Library and Information Science,* Vol. 7 (New York:

Marcel Dekker, 1972), pp. 69-120.
(*See* E 5.7)

1315   Wessel, C. J.
"Environmental factors affecting the permanence of library materials."
Library Quarterly 40 (January 1970): 39-84.
(*See* B 1.2)

1316   Weyde, E.
"A simple test to identify gases which destroy silver images."
Photographic Science and Engineering 16, 4 (1972): 283-86.

1317   Whalley, J. I.
Writing Implements and Accessories, From the Roman Stylus to the Typewriter.
Newton Abbott, England: David and Charles, 1975.

Wheatley, C. J.
See 939, Oddy, W. A.

1318   "When books are water-soaked there's an emergency treatment."
Wyoming Library Roundup 30 (September 1975): 12-13.

1319   Whipkey, H. E.
After Agnes: A report on Flood Recovery Assistance by the Pennsylvania Historical and Museum Commission.
Harrisburg, Pennsylvania: Pennsylvania Historical and Museum Commission, 1973.

1320   "Who—or what—shall live? Preservationists confer."
American Libraries 8 (February 1977): 61.

1321   Wieder, J.
"Erfahrungen einer flutkatastrophe; die reorganization der Florentiner nationalbibliothek" ("Experiences of a flood catastrophe; the reorganization of the Florentine national library").

Zeitschrift für Bibliothekswesen und Bibliographie 15,
1 (1968): 1-16.

1322   Wieder, J.
"Internationale zusammenarbeit auf dem gebiet der
konservierung und restaurierung von bibliotheksgut;
bericht über das Florentiner kolloquium vom 12.-14.
Marz 1970" ("International cooperation in the field of
conservation and restoration of library materials; report
on the colloquium held in Florence, March 12-14,
1970").
Zeitschrift für Bibliothekswesen und Bibliographie 17,
6 (1970): 401-405.

1323   Wieder, J.
"The restoration and conservation of library and archive
materials as an international task."
IFLA Journal 1, 1 (1975): 21-29.
(*See* A 4.7)

1324   Wieder, J.
"Unesco seminar on international co-operation in the
field of book and document preservation, Florence,
March 12-14, 1970."
IFLA News 33 (July 1970): 6-7.

1325   Wiest, D. G.
"Film, the durable medium."
Special Libraries 62 (November 1971): 475-80.

1326   Wilhelm, H.
Preservation of Contemporary Photographic Materials.
Grinnell, Iowa: East Street Gallery.
Forthcoming.

Wilkinson, I. B.
See 967, Pearson, V.; 1172, Stolow, N.

1327   Willey, A. E.
"The Charles Klein Law Library fire."
Fire Journal 66, 6 (November 1972): 16-22.

1328   Williams, E. E.
       "Deterioration of library collections today."
       Library Quarterly 40 (January 1970): 3-17.

1329   Williams, G.
       "The preservation of deteriorating books; examination
       of the problem."
       Library Journal 91 (January 1, 1966): 51-56.
       (*See* A 1.8)

1330   Williams, G.
       "The preservation of deteriorating books; recommenda-
       tions for a solution."
       Library Journal 91 (January 15, 1966): 189-94.
       (*See* A 1.8)

1331   Williams, G.
       "Specifications for permanent/durable paper for carbon
       copies."
       American Archivist 35 (January 1972): 81-85.
       (Technical notes)

1332   Williams, J. C.
       "Chemistry of the deacidification of paper."
       *International Institute for Conservation of Historic and
       Artistic Works, Bulletin of the American Group* 12, 1
       (1971): 16-32.

1333   Williams, J. C., ed.
       *Preservation of Paper and Textiles of Historical and
       Artistic Value.*
       Washington, D. C.: American Chemical Society, 1977.
       (Advances in Chemistry Series, no. 164)
       (*See also* articles from this work, cited separately, by
       G. M. Cunha,   D. J. Fischer,   G. B. Kelley,   B. C.
       Middleton,   R. Perkinson, R. D. Smith, R. A. Stuhrke,
       and B. Walker.)
       (*See* E 3.1)

1334   Williams, J. C., and G. B. Kelley.
       "Research on mass treatments in conservation."
       *Bulletin of the American Institute for Conservation of
       Historic and Artistic Works*   14, 2 (1974): 69-77.

1335 Williams, J. C., and G. B. Kelley.
      "Research on mass treatments in conservation."
      *Bulletin of the American Institute for Conservation of
      Historic and Artistic Works* 14, 2 (1974): 69-77.

1336 Williams, J. C., and others.
      "Metal catalysts in the oxidative degradation of paper."
      In *Preservation of Paper and Textiles of Historical and
      Artistic Value* (Washington, D. C.: American Chemical
      Society, 1977), pp. 37-61.
      (Advances in Chemistry Series, no. 164)

1337 Willison, I. R.
      "The intrusive lens."
      TLS 3947 (November 18, 1977): 3958.

1338 Wilson, A. G.
      "Ventilation and air quality."
      Canadian Building Digest no. 110 (February 1969).

1339 Wilson, W. K.
      "New approaches to preservation: discussion."
      Library Quarterly 40 (January 1970): 171-75.

1340 Wilson, W. K.
      "Record papers and their preservation."
      Chemistry 43 (March 1970).

1341 Wilson, W. K., and J. L. Gear.
      Care of Books, Documents, Prints and Films.
      Washington, D. C.: U. S. Department of Commerce,
      National Bureau of Standards, 1971.
      (NBS consummer information series 5)

1342 Wilson, W. K., and R. L. Hebert.
      "Evaluation of the Stability of record papers."
      Tappi 52 (1969): 1523-29.

1343 Wilson, W. K., M. C. McKiel, J. L. Gear, and R. H.
      MacClaren.
      "Preparation of solutions of magnesium bicarbonate for
      deacidification."
      American Archivist 41 (January 1978): 67-70.

1344   Wilson, W. K., and E. J. Parks.
        Development of Specifications for Archival Record Materials.
        Washington, D. C.: Paper Evaluation Section, Institute for Materials Research, National Bureau of Standards, 1973.
        (*See also American Archivist* 33 (April 1970): 219-33. Technical notes)

1345   Wingate, R. B.
        "Kitchen chemistry in the care of books."
        AB Bookman's Weekly 59 (June 6, 1977): 3506-3509.
        (*See* subsequent issues for lively discussions.)

        Wingate, R. B.
        See 814, Mortimer, R.; 539, Hey, M.

1346   Winger, H. W., and R. D. Smith, eds.
        Deterioration and Preservation of Library Materials; the Thirty-fourth Annual Conference of the Graduate Library School; August 4-6, 1969.
        Chicago: University of Chicago Press, 1970.
        Published originally in *Library Quarterly* 40 (January 1970).
        (*See* E 5.8)

        Wink, W. A.
        See 194, Browning, B. L.

1347   Wittig, D.
        "Preservation of library materials was given critical attention at the New York Library Association's 77th annual conference."
        Library of Congress Information Bulletin 30 (February 4, 1971): 74-75.

1348   Wood, R. D., and Mrs. E. D. Shorland.
        "The daguerreotype portrait of Dorothy Draper."
        Photographic Journal 110 (December 1970): 478-82.

1349   Woodhouse, A. J.
"The Queensland State Archives fumigation unit;
ethylene oxide/vacuum fumigation as an aid for the
preservation of archives and manuscripts."
Archives and Manuscripts 4 (November 1970): 14-20.

1350   "Workshops for librarians help to maintain library
volumes."
Library Scene 5 (September 1976): 30.

1351   Wright, A. E.
"Prices up, quality down, workmanship shoddy."
Publishers' Weekly 207 (January 6, 1975): 10.
(letter)

1352   Wright, J. C.
"Conservation of library materials: problems and
prospects."
Hawaii Library Association Journal 29, 1 (June 1972):
3-6.

1353   "Writings on archives, historical manuscripts, and current
records."
In *American Archivist* (annual)

1354   Wrotenbery, C. R.
"Recovery from disaster: the University of Corpus
Christi Library recovers from Hurricane Celia."
In Cunha, G. M., and N. P. Tucker, eds., *Library and
Archives Conservation: The Boston Athenaeum's 1971
Seminar on the Application of Chemical and Physical
Methods to the Conservation of Library and Archival
Materials: May 17-21, 1971* (Boston: The Library of
the Boston Athenaeum, 1972), pp. 221-227.

XYZ

1355 Yerkes, C. P.
"Paper shortage: an outlook for the microfilm industry."
Information: Part 1 6 (March 1974): 76-78.
Also published in *Journal of Micrographics* 7 (March 1974): 143-46.

1356 Yoho, C. H., and T. W. Riley.
"Fire protection of records by the use of high expansion foam."
Records Management Quarterly 10 (April 1976): 16-19.

Young, F. J.
See 275, Collings, T. J.

1357 Young, L. C.
Materials in Printing Processes.
New York: Hastings House, 1973.

1358 Young, R. F.
"American bookbinder's work in Florence; a brief account of his experiences."
Library of Congress Information Bulletin 27 (April 25, 1968): 231-232.
Also published under the title "Second apprenticeship."
AB Bookman's Weekly 41 (April 29, 1968): 1659-60.

1359 Young, W. J.
"Florence flood, November 4, 1965; some notes and recollections."
Boston Museum Bulletin 66, 345 (1968): 101-115.

1360 Yuill, P. J.
"Preservation proposals."
School Library Journal 23 (September 1976): 3.
(letter)

1361   Zappalà Plossi, M.
"Aspetti attuali della ricerca chimica nell'Istituto di Patologia del Libro" ("Current chemical research in the Institute of Book Pathology").
Bollettino dell'Instituto di Patologia del Libro   31 (January-December 1972): 153-165.

1362   Zentralinstitut für Bibliothekswesen.
Buchpflegefibel; ein Ratgeber für allgemeinbildende Bibliotheken ("Primer of book care; a guide of public libraries").
Leipzig: Bibliographisches Institut, 1967.
3d ed.

1363   Zhvirblis, I.
"Polimernye plenki sokhraniaiut knigi" ("Polymer film preserves books").
Bibliotekar' no. 4 (1972): 61.

1364   Zigrosser, C., and C. M. Gaehde.
A Guide to the Collecting and Care of Original Prints. New York: Crown Publishers for the Print Council of America, 1965.

1365   Zittel, B.
"Der Grossband aus der Burg Trausnitz in Landshut: Erfahrungen und Lehren" ("The fire at the Trausnitz Castle: experiences and lessons").
Archivalische Zeitschrift 61 (1965): 142-92.
Abstract in *American Archivist* 30 (October 1967): 609-610.

1366   Zucker, H.
"Old-time processes—how to identify and date them."
Popular Photography, December 1972, 99-101, 170, 216.

1367   Zuker, J.
"Ralph Sargents' *Preserving the Moving Image:* a summary review."
In Perry, T., ed., *Performing Arts Resources, Volume 2* (New York: Drama Specialists/Publishers, 1975), pp. 15-29.

Subject Index